AFRICAN
AMERICAN
Special Days

AFRICAN
AMERICAN
Special Days

Cheryl A. Kirk-Duggan

ABINGDON PRESS
NASHVILLE

AFRICAN AMERICAN SPECIAL DAYS

Copyright © 1996 by Cheryl A. Kirk-Duggan

This book is printed on acid-free, recycled paper.

Library of Congress Cataloging-in-Publication Data

Kirk-Duggan, Cheryl A.
    African American special days / Cheryl A. Kirk-Duggan.
        p.   cm.
    ISBN 0-687-00920-0 (pbk. : alk. paper)
    1. Afro-Americans—Religion.   2. Fasts and feasts.   I. Title.
    BR563.N4K57   1996
    263'.97'08996073—dc20   96-16085
                                                                                            CIP

Scripture quotations, unless otherwise noted, are from the New Revised Standard Version of the Bible, copyright © 1989 by the Division of Christian Education of the National Council of the Churches of Christ in the USA. Used by permission.

00 01 02 03 04 05 — 10 9 8 7 6 5 4

MANUFACTURED IN THE UNITED STATES OF AMERICA

CONTENTS

◇◇◇

ACKNOWLEDGMENTS

$\mathcal{G}$rowing up in a Black church shaped my entire life. I was nurtured through Sunday school, Bible school, Bible study, conventions, district and annual conferences, leadership training schools and programs. All my family members—from my maternal grandmother, Rebecca Mosely Brooks; my parents, the late Rudolph Valentino and Naomi Ruth Mosely Kirk; aunts; uncles; siblings; cousins (three and four times removed)—were and are active in Reeves Temple. My gratitude to those who have shaped my creativity, values, and strengths. My conversation with Hal Kildahl, at the American Academy of Religion and Society of Biblical Literature (AAR/SBL) annual meeting in 1993, and the humor and editorial support of my husband, Michael A. Kirk-Duggan, are the impetus for writing this book.

INTRODUCTION

*B*lack folk like to celebrate. Religious occasions are eminently important celebrations that are accomplished with beauty and purpose. My life reflects celebration and vitality among Black folk in church. I sang my first solo at age four, "Take the Name of Jesus with You," in the Junior Choir at Reeves Temple Christian Methodist Episcopal Church, Lake Charles, Louisiana. I began piano lessons at age five, which later made possible my first opportunity for employment. In the summer of my eleventh year, I became the pianist for my church's children's choir. Shortly thereafter, I experienced baptism by fire on a First Sunday Morning, the day our church celebrated the Lord's Supper. The regular organist was ill, and someone said to me: "Play the organ this morning!" When I persisted, saying, "I've had only a few lessons," the good saint said, "Play anyway!"

Later I became one of the church's organists. By the time I graduated from high school, I had played for hundreds of services and had worked with many choirs. I have never stopped playing: through four academic degrees, a call and an ordination to ministry. Thus, not only can I measure my life experience since I have known music, but also that music knowledge simultaneously deals with my recognition of the reality of God at work in my own life and in the life of the Black church.

This volume is a tool to enhance Black church programming and to reflect the elegant, faith-seeking, life-affirming, and freedom-longing people that we are. Each special day provides these elements: (a) occasion; (b) welcome; (c) prayer; (d) litany; (e) vow of commitment; (f) suggested colors and scriptures; and (g) poem of reflection.

The layout of each service is based on scripture and the African American life experience and history. The selected scriptures embrace a psalm, an Old Testament reading, a Gospel, and an Epistle, with a focus on love, service or worship, commitment or trust, as well as God's gifts to us. Where possible, I use African American persons to illustrate an attitude or commitment. These program helps bring together the worship experience and our Black heritage, and are a tool to instill esteem and inspiration for religious, spiritual, and general education purposes. Most of the statements and prayers provide spaces to insert the names of the church, related dates or numbers, and/or geographical places. These statements and prayers can be tailored for your own church ceremony by including the names of honorees, the community, or of helpful members where appropriate.

These services can be used as they appear here or selected portions can be included in other program formats. For example, use the suggested colors in program design (e.g., in the colors for flowers, candles, bulletin board decorations, publicity, and the attire for the service). Incorporate the suggested scripture, in whole or in part, in the body of the program as a resource for theme development, or as tools for spiritual reflection and team building for the overall program committee.

I submit these prayers, litanies, statements, and ideas in a prayerful spirit of love for your use and to God's glory.

Advent 1995

CHILDREN AND YOUTH DAYS

Occasion

Jesus said: "Let the little children come to me, and do not stop them; for it is to such as these that the kingdom (the rule) of God belongs" (Matt. 19:14-15; Luke 18:15-17; Mark 10:13-16). Jesus blesses children and youth. He teaches that we all come to God's kingdom as children. This means that we simply need to depend on and trust in God. Today we celebrate Jesus and rejoice that he blesses us and that children and youth are gifts. Today we also challenge the [*church name*] family, parents, guardians, immediate and extended family members to love, support, teach, and be role models to our children and youth.

God calls us to teach by example. We, the children and youth of [church name], need you to teach us how to respect ourselves and others. Please take time for us and discipline us through the love of Christ. Children are rare and precious gems. Each child is unique and has special, God-given talents and gifts. We pray that God blesses all of us and that our parents and guardians will love us and provide a spiritual, creative, challenging environment where we can blossom. We thank God for the chance to be Christian children, youth, and adults.

Welcome

O magnify the Lord! With the joy and innocence of children and youth, we welcome each of you to this wonderful celebration of Christian life. To the pastor, officers, members, and friends of [church name], we bring you greetings! The children and youth departments are excited about our God-given gifts and opportunities. We consider it an honor to be in charge of the services and we welcome and invite each of you to join in and participate with us. Make yourselves comfortable in the Lord.

We offer our praises, songs, prayers, and readings as a joyful noise unto the Lord. Help us celebrate! Clap your hands, tap your feet if the Lord moves you in that way. We welcome you with open hands and hearts, to experience God in this holy sanctuary. Each of us is God's child; for God created all of us. As we are made in God's image, we are to bear witness to the world. So being that witness, today we invite you to praise God and be so inspired that this joy brings you closer to God and to knowing yourself. Welcome.

Prayer

Dear Jesus, O how we love you! We know that you love us; that your life teaches us how to live. You gave your life for us that we might have life more abundantly. Lord, we thank you, so much, for caring for us. We know you are our shepherd and guide, even when we are overwhelmed, and when life is confusing. Sometimes we are afraid. Sometimes we make mistakes. Sometimes we disobey our parents and teachers. Many times we think we can do things differently because we are young. Often we do our best and it is not enough or people do not seem to care. Many times we do not understand our parents, our feelings, or our world.

Lord, we know that you love us in good times and in bad. You are our guide, and you give our pastors, parents, and leaders insight and wisdom to help us. Lord, be with us as we communicate with other children, youth, and adults. Lord, please guide the leaders of our families, church, schools, community, and the world; help them be good stewards of all our resources. Help them create a world that is safe for us. Help us to learn, grow, and be like you in all we say and do. Help us to be strong and not let peer pressure force us to do bad things. Lord, help us to appreciate our gifts, families, and ourselves. We thank you, O God, for life and for all creation. Amen.

Litany

LEADER: Jesus loves us! We love Jesus! The Bible tells us to love the Lord, our God, and to love our neighbors as ourselves.

PEOPLE: **We celebrate God's gracious and merciful love for us: that love is for all the children of the world. Let us be like God and love one another.**

LEADER: The love of God is unconditional, slow to anger and always listens. God's love enables us to live every day, to build communities and friendships.

PEOPLE: God's love helps us to grow up to respect ourselves and others, and to see our lives as part of God's rule, God's kingdom.

LEADER: God's love, wisdom, and knowledge guides our parents and teachers to lead us and teach us in the way we should go, so when we are old we will not depart from it.

PEOPLE: The children and youth are our heritage, our wealth, and our joy. May we love and respect our offspring, and instruct them so that they may live to be loving, responsible adults.

ALL: By God's faith and grace, we grow and mature; we experience God's loving salvation and become new creatures in Christ Jesus: one body, one church, one faith, one Lord.

Vow of Commitment

We, the children (and youth) of [*church name*], stand before God and the church to recommit our lives to be like Jesus. We want to walk in the light, the beautiful light of Jesus so that we can let our lights shine. Our light is the light of the Lord in us.

We pledge to let our light shine daily as we do our best at home, school, church, at work, and at play. We will respect others and ourselves. We will practice obedience and discipline in our relationships and our activities, in study and in play. With the Lord as our helper, we will study the Bible and use it as our guide. We thank God for our talents and gifts, for the ability to create, read, think, learn, dream dreams, and have visions of greatness.

Hallelujah for the goodness, joy, and blessings of light. We want to be all that God created us to be. God's free gift of grace helps us and guides us in our worship and work, and helps us to trust and obey as we serve our Lord. We can make a difference. We pledge to share the Lord with others and bring the light of Jesus to dark places.

Suggested Colors

The colors for children and youth day are yellow and green. Yellow symbolizes joy, good cheer, spring, warmth, wisdom, knowledge, intelligence, and inspiration. Green depicts life, love, rebirth, the power of nature, freshness, healing, peace, and the divine.

Scriptures

Lord, you have been our dwelling place in all generations. Before the mountains were brought forth, or ever you had formed the earth and the world, from everlasting to everlasting, you are God. (Ps. 90:1-2)

The wolf shall live with the lamb, the leopard shall lie down with the kid, the calf and the lion and the fatling together, and a little child shall lead them. (Isa. 11: 6)

"And my spirit rejoices in God my Savior." (Luke 1: 47)

So we can say with confidence, "The Lord is my helper; I will not be afraid. What can anyone do to me?" (Heb. 13: 6)

Poem of Reflection

OUR CHILDREN, OUR WEALTH

How blessed are we:
God gives us children
To love and cherish,
To nurture and take care of.
What a challenge,
What a joy,
Exciting, interesting, difficult
Always a blessing.

Children: young, teen, older,
All ways our children;
Made in God's image,
Our heritage.
Their ideas, their creativity

Their warmth and our concern
Their traits, their looks
Their habits, our needs,
Our children are us.

We spread the Word of Jesus to our children.
Our children grow, love, live in faith,
Experience this world
Know God
Love and are loved.
Our children,
Our abundance,
Our freedom,
Our love.

SUNDAY SCHOOL CONVENTIONS AND YOUTH CONFERENCES

Occasion

The Wisdom book of Proverbs teaches us to "train children in the right way, and when old, they will not stray" (22:6). Today we celebrate the sacredness of children, youth, young adults, adults, and the divine edict to nurture, love, and educate them. The members of [*name of church or convention*] are our heritage and strength, our jewels, our legacy. Each of us are children in God's eyes. We are growing and are called to be in a renewing, loving relationship with God. God created us in God's own image. This creation makes us sacred beings, for we belong to God. Today we celebrate the innocence of that sacredness. We honor the love and respect for one another that Jesus talks about as he says, "Love the Lord your God with all your heart, and with all your soul, and with all your mind. . . . You shall love your neighbor as yourself" (Matt. 22:37, 39).

We respect the ministry of communication about God's love, forgiveness, redemption, and reconciliation toward critical thinking where students, teachers, and advisers are mutual partners. We honor the mission of [*Sunday schools or youth ministries*] as they provide a place of learning scripture and experiencing Christian nurture. We recognize the importance of teaching and receiving information about the revelation of God as God acts throughout history. We celebrate the commitment of the church family to provide an environment where we all teach by what we do and we all learn by what we see.

We cherish the earnest love and commitment pledge of [*Sunday school teachers, superintendents, or youth counselors*] as they minister with love, discipline, and compassion. We thank God for the children, youth, young adults, and adults gathered here and for the ministry of Christian education.

Welcome

God calls us to be a living, forgiving, Christ-centered community shaped by love. Today we share that blessed love with you. In the spirit of love, we welcome each of you to [*name of convention, Sunday school, or church*]. On behalf of the pastor [*or leader*], officers, and members, we extend our hospitality to you. Our [*youth department or Sunday school*] is our asset and our legacy. In celebrating this department, we affirm our part in honoring God's call on the church to nurture our young. God founded the church as a loving witness to the revealed divine love and power of true humanity expressed through Jesus Christ.

People are the church: the church strongly relies on our children, youth, young adults, and adults right now! The [*children and/or youth and/or adults*] of [*name of church or convention name*] stand together and take our place in this church and community as members and leaders have before us. We welcome you to join with us and participate with us as a community of faith called to learn, to know wisdom and joy. We invite you to unite with us in the worship of God in this sacred place and then carry the message beyond these doors.

We all stand in the traditions of those who have stood for truth and justice—of the children, youth, young adults, and adults who have worked toward freedom, justice, and the education of all. Today we salute the educational ministry of the [*church name*] family. We honor this legacy, from the early slave church in the hush or bush arbors (secret, well-hidden areas amid bushes and undergrowth) to the sacrifice of the four little girls—Denise McNair, Addie Mae Collins, Carol Robinson, and Cynthia Wesley—who died in the 1964 bombing of the Sixteenth Street Baptist Church in Birmingham, to those who today volunteer at church and church-related ministries. These ministries include activities as diverse as tutoring and voter registration to HIV prevention and sponsoring of programming for our elegant senior members. May you be blessed and inspired by your presence here. Again, welcome.

Prayer

O God, our Parent and Friend, we give you all praise and honor. Dearest Shepherd, you are so gentle and loving with us. Your mercy is ever present even as you judge us. You have given us rule over all things; you have blessed us with minds to think and be creative. Great Teacher, you give us bodies to run and jump, to experience the grandness of creation. Lord, we bless and thank you for your great bounty.

Help us, dear Creator, to accept the challenge of the gospel and of history. Help us to communicate and to live steeped in divine wisdom. Bless our gathering with a spirit of unity, grace, and joy. May our moments together be rich with teaching and learning about you and ourselves. Guide us and our leaders, loving God, that we might grow in love and strength that gives us the courage to minister wherever we may be. Come, Holy Spirit! Open our minds and hearts that we may receive Holy Scriptures to the edification of ourselves, our church, our community. Lord, we ask you to teach us how to pray, how to live, for you only are God. Today we humbly ask that you teach us how to exchange knowledge: to teach, learn, interpret, and apply divine information and experience of the heart to our daily lives. All honor, glory, and power are yours. Amen.

Litany

LEADER: Rejoice that God brings us together to celebrate through activities of praise, education, and fellowship. We come with thankful hearts that [*church, district, or organization name*] has set aside this time to honor our contribution and sharing in the church family.

PEOPLE: **Indeed we lift our voices in glad hosannas. This is our time to talk about our relationship with God, and about some of the ways we study and interact, as we declare our membership in the Body of Christ.**

LEADER: Humbly we stand before the Lord, with family and friends in joy. Many among us know sorrow; others are searching for answers and seeking to understand mysteries. For the comfort of membership and the support felt by all, we give thanks.

PEOPLE: **We affirm that Christ's call on our lives concerns our individual and communal salvation. We are called to witness by our lives of the power of God's grace.**

Through classes, workshops, and Bible study, we learn God's Word—the spiritual food that energizes our daily lives. God's Word teaches us how to participate in group activities as members of God's worshiping family.

LEADER: We look to Jesus Christ as our model for true humanity—teacher, student, leader, and friend. Jesus accepted the call on his life at an early age. As an adult, Jesus fed the hungry, healed the sick, and preached good news to sinners. Jesus continues to lead us like a shepherd and calls us to active love, learning, and sharing.

ALL: **Help us dear Savior, in our studies and activities—at school, work, play, or church to listen well, act lovingly, think clearly, and speak graciously.**

Vow of Commitment

We, the members of the [*name of group or organization*] stand to rededicate our lives to daily walk with Christ. What we do reflects what we study and what we say: our daily study of scripture, our prayer life, and our everyday activity. We want to be faithful, honest, and true to ourselves, our church community, and our Lord. We confess that many times we sin, even when we try to do good. We are grateful that you never stop loving us, and that you temper your judgment with mercy. Your forgiving nature and loving-kindness inspire us to let our commitment to Christ Jesus radiate wherever we go. As you beckon us to follow you, we accept the challenge of living a Christian life with humility and gratitude. We recommit all our energies, artistic gifts, and talents to serve and support God's rule on earth.

We appreciate, O God, your gift of life. We accept the challenge to respect ourselves in every way: to treat and honor our bodies, minds, and spirits like we treat your temple, O Lord. Through your grace, we can be good students and loving role models to our younger sisters and brothers. In gratitude and humility, we celebrate the sacredness of our lives and of the call you have on us. All glory and honor be yours. May you be blessed and let us daily be open to your blessing. Amen.

Suggested Colors

Green and white are the suggested colors for Sunday school conventions and youth workshops or conferences. Green symbolizes new growth, fresh ideas, development, nurturing, learning environments, freshness, healing, peace, the divine, and elegance. White, not a color in itself but a combination of the colors of the rainbow, symbolizes purity, peace, light, and illumination.

Scriptures

O my God, in you [we] trust; do not let [us] be put to shame; do not let [our] enemies exult over [us]. (Ps. 25:2)

From new moon to new moon, and from sabbath to sabbath, all flesh shall come to worship before me, says the LORD. *(Isa. 66:23)*

"But I [Jesus] say to you that listen, Love your enemies, do good to those who hate you." (Luke 6:27)

For I [Paul] am longing to see you so that I may share with you some spiritual gift to strengthen you—or rather so that we may be mutually encouraged by each other's faith, both yours and mine. (Rom. 1:11-12)

Poem of Reflection

CONVENTIONS: HALLELUJAH MEETING TIME

Hallelujah, it's church meeting time!
Sunday school or district conventions
We're packed and ready to go!
Ready to go and praise God's name!
Ready to see friends from last year,
Ready to show what we have learned,
Ready to grow some more.

Hallelujah! Hallelujah!
The music is so grand.
Ladies and gents dressed to the nines;

Ushers at attention—
Youth ministers preparing to preach,
Gospel bird frying,
Dressing, greens, and sweet potato pie
Homemade ice cream on the side.

It's convention time;
Welcomes are made,
Sweet smells in the air,
Music is great;
Word stands sure;
Sermons prepared;
Uniforms and robes pressed,
Church house cleaned,
Jesus is here!
Oh, what a time!
What a time, indeed!

GRADUATION
AND PROMOTION DAYS

Occasion

Recognition is honorable and helps us to highlight the milestones in our lives. In joy, we celebrate [*graduation or promotion*] of the [*name of the classes or group*] of [*name of church or organization*]. Many steps make up the ladder of achievement. That process involves work and much effort by the faculty, staff, and the supportive members of [*church or community*].

The knowledge gained and the lessons learned are tools that help us to be more loving, more Christlike. Today we celebrate all efforts made to nurture and prepare our [*graduates or students being promoted*]. This occasion honors the successful. Every time we study God's Word and exercise our understanding in our daily lives we are a success. Education is an act of grace: a gift of God's loving-kindness that can give us insight and joyfulness.

Joyfulness comes as we appreciate people and the gifts of goods and events in our lives. Joyfulness reflects the wonder and awesomeness we encounter as we realize God is for us and with us. The possibilities and enlightenment that occur through the education process show God being with us in concern and love. We take the mantle of education and scholarship in the church and the world and salute those African Americans who have paved the way for us in history and recently: Anna Julia Cooper, scholar; Mary McCleod Bethune, educator and activist; George Washington Carver, scientist and inventor; Richard Allen and Absalom Jones, AME and AMEZ founding bishops; Cornel West, author and philosopher; Henry L. Gates, literary critic; Samuel Proctor, pastor and professor; Calvin Butts, pastor and activist; James H. Cone, theologian; Barbara Harris, Anglican bishop; Jacquelyn Grant, womanist scholar and theologian; Katie Cannon, womanist scholar and ethicist; Johnnetta Coles and Marguerite Ross Barnett, university presidents. [*Include current leaders in your own denominational churches and schools and pertinent secular Black schools.*]

We also honor the work and lives of [*name of local and state workers in Christian and secular education*]. Their labors and their students' work make this day possible. Education does not mean we are better than others and does not allow us to judge others. Education is a tool for enlightenment and improving the plight of ourselves and others. We take seriously the process of developing the knowledge, the skill, and the mental, spiritual, and emotional characters of all teachers and students to the honor and glory of God. Praise and thanksgiving! Hallelujah!

Welcome

The psalmist cries out words of gladness in praise of Zion in Psalm 122. The group of pilgrims arrive in Jerusalem and rejoice at the unity the buildings symbolize. We honor and greet all of you whose pilgrimage has allowed you to bless us with your presence. We rejoice that the Lord has brought us together in unity to celebrate [*graduation of promotion*] day. We receive you in gladness and cordiality with open hearts. The pastor, leaders, officers, members, and friends of [*church name or organization*] invite you to participate with us as we honor the [*graduates or students promoted*] this year from [*name of class or church school*].

These students represent the beautiful, the good, and the true in our lives. We are beautiful for we are God's children. We are good in that God made us that way in the beginning and we are called to do good things. One way we know truth is through Christ Jesus. We know truth and beauty as we use all our God-given gifts to help us actively love and make a difference. We welcome you here! We welcome you to explore the good, true, and beautiful within because Christ is here in us and with us. Welcome.

Prayer

We come as an extended family, to offer praise and thanksgiving for the commitment represented here. We thank you, O God, our Supreme Teacher, for the ministry of church and academic education. We bless your precious name, and ask that you bless those who continuously give and receive knowledge. Help us to appreciate the gifts and marvels of learning and enlightenment. Help us to see that education is a lifelong process that informs all areas of our life.

Lord, we know you hear each idea and concept spoken in your name and each heart that cries out for answers. Help us to think through and ask the questions that help us function lovingly in society toward our sisters and brothers in Christ Jesus.

Help us to study and apply your Word that we may have wisdom and integrity in our beliefs and ethical practices. Help us to take seriously and become actively involved in the education of our children and youth: by showing our children that we love them; by providing an environment that is safe and conducive to study; by teaching our children to read, write, and do math early on; by regularly visiting schools and being active in parent-teacher associations and in our church's Christian education program; by monitoring homework and being interested in the course of studies; by emphasizing scripture and African American life experiences and heritage daily; by seeing parenting and education as a ministry. For this insight and all other blessings, we thank you. Amen.

Litany

LEADER: O Divine Teacher and Redeemer, we rejoice and are glad for the gifts of knowledge that this day brings and celebrates.

PEOPLE: **In gracious joy, we lift our voices to proclaim our delight in your many gifts of knowledge and experience. We honor the accomplishments of those recipients who have gone the distance and accomplished much.**

LEADER: We offer thanks for the gifts of hearing, sight, touch, taste, and smell that strengthen and enhance our education process.

PEOPLE: Dear Creator, we thank you for the call you place on our lives to minister to others through teaching and sharing knowledge.

LEADER: Help us to be so grateful for our education that we encourage those who teach and preach; and we inspire others to write our stories, to create, to invent, to start businesses, to learn.

PEOPLE: We shout hosannas! As we gain knowledge, we experience the truth of Christ, and that truth will set us free.

ALL: God anoints us and sends us out in truth as disciples and ministers of the Word of Jesus Christ, through the power of the Holy Spirit. We accept the challenge and choose to learn and to celebrate the milestones of learning with the household of faith: the community of believers in Christ Jesus.

Vow of Commitment

Lord God of Deborah and Solomon, teacher of teachers and creator of leaders: we honor the giving and receiving of knowledge and the opportunity to celebrate Christian achievement. In gratitude for your grace that has instituted this program of study, we pledge to excel as we continue to teach and learn wherever our faith journey takes us.

We bless you, O God, for bringing us thus far on our educational journey. We accept your challenge to mold our lives in the ways of Christ: to be disciples and to disciple others. We pledge to use the knowledge and skills received this year in ministry. May we learn and live by the Christian biblical and life principles taught during the [name of class or group] at [church name]. We are grateful to [names of teachers, *sponsors, superintendents, pastors*]. In honor of their contributions, nurture, and care, we rededicate our lives to God's service. We vow to continue our studies and association with [*name of class or group*]. We confess the experience of grace afforded by the relationships built through group study and the empowerment born of new knowledge. May the Grand Architect of the universe and of all knowledge keep us and protect us.

Suggested Colors

White and purple are the suggested colors for graduation. White symbolizes purity, peace, light, and illumination. Purple depicts royalty, penitence, power, self-esteem, and depth of feeling.

Scriptures

[Lord], [we are] your servant[s]; give [us] understanding, so that [we] may know your decrees. (Ps. 119:125)

They do not know, nor do they comprehend; for their eyes are shut, so that they cannot see, and their minds as well, so that they cannot understand. (Isa. 44:18)

And they came and said to him, "[Jesus], we know that you are sincere, and show deference to no one; for you do not regard people with partiality, but teach the way of God in accordance with truth." (Mark 12:14a)

To one is given through the Spirit the utterance of wisdom, and to another the utterance of knowledge according to the same Spirit. (1 Cor. 12:8)

Poem of Reflection

GRADUATION AND PROMOTION DAYS

Certificates and diplomas
Announce to the world
The hard work and dedication of
Families and friends
Students and educators:
To better ourselves
And the rest of humanity
For the glory of God.

Ideas, concepts, thoughts,
Visions, drawings, experiments,
Speeches, poems, essays,
Athletic events, a collegiate bowl,
Express part of us
Express part of God
In whose image we are made.

Let's honor education,
Not make it a god.
Let's work passionately,
Let's do well:
Shunning attitudes of
Superiority or judgment.

God's Grace
Bestows our gifts,
Behooves us to excel,
To feel good about ourselves:
With gratitude and purpose,
Share what we have,
Never stop learning,
Never stop caring,
Dream dreams,
Plan well,
Work hard,
Share God.

HOMECOMING
AND FAMILY REUNIONS

Occasion

Family and community building are central to African American life. Extended family existed in Africa, during slavery, and continues today. Blood defines only some of our kinships. We have "cousins," "aunts," and "uncles" through association. With gratitude and joy, we, the members of [*name of the group, family, and/or church family*], remember all of our kinfolk as we observe this [*homecoming or family reunion*].

Family and community building involve sharing and togetherness through God's benevolent grace. Today, we honor the virtues and activities that keep and have kept us, despite the Middle Passage, slavery, northern and western migration, and Jim Crow. We celebrate the wisdom that created a meal out of pot liquor, greens, and hoecake—the cuisine known as soul food. We champion the spirit that let us take in family, friends, and neighbor's children without needing state action. We celebrate the unity that let our mothers and their mothers come together and make warm quilts out of rags and old clothes. We thank God for fathers and mothers who sacrificed for us, who held down many jobs to feed us, educated us in the Lord, and who survived.

We celebrate the vision of those who started our historic Black colleges; we honor the purposefulness of Black leadership from the Underground Railroad through and beyond the Civil Rights movement. We cherish those noble saints who wage war against sin, abuse, addiction, crime. We admire those who volunteer in religious and civic programs, those who see parenting and friendship as ministry.

We bless God for the institution of family, especially for our children and our elders who know God, speak truth, and show us how to love. Today we celebrate family unity and love: a structure branded as one in the spirit of Christ Jesus.

Welcome

"I was glad when they said to me, 'Let us go to the house of the LORD!'" (Ps. 122:1). We know gladness because we are called to praise God. Today, we, the pastors, officers, and members of [church name] and the [name of homecoming or family reunion group], are glad to welcome you to praise the Lord, be restored, and to experience renewal and recommitment as we honor the [homecoming or family reunion] of [church name or name of family]. The power of love and togetherness is the foundation of this worship service. Through God's grace the [offspring of the family name] or [members of the group or organization] are here as a testament of the faith and hope of God's people. With anticipating spirits and joyful hearts, we invite you to be here with us, participate, and have a good time.

On behalf of [*church, organization, or family name*], we embrace you in Christ's love. We hold true to the communal spirit long since forged in the slave church of the bush arbor (secret, well-hidden areas amid bushes and undergrowth), the extended family, and the early Christian church. We invite you to embrace that spirit at church, home, work, and play. We welcome you to the profound experience of being with the Body of Christ. Be welcome. Be well. Be a part of our family. Welcome.

Prayer

O majestic, divine Creator of the universe, who rules wind and water, who created the sparrow, the rose, the whale; who created us: we come in jubilance, asking you to bless this [*homecoming or reunion*] service done in your honor, to your glory.

Dearest Lily of the Valley, be our source and guide. Help us to grow and be flowers of beauty and peace. Help us to be true families—spreading love and actively communicating by being good listeners and clear speakers, saying what we mean in love.

O God, we acknowledge the presence of powers and principalities. Like Paul, when we desire to do good, we often do evil. In seeing our faults, O Bright and Morning Star, help us to see the goodness that you placed in us at creation. Help us to grow and be true to you in families and groups that will enable us to be Jesus to all we meet. Help us to be honest, to offer forgiveness. Please heal our wounds and make us whole; let us listen so that our words and actions are spiritually healthy.

We rejoice in the gifts of life, creativity, love, joy, and hope. Lord, anoint those gathered here to do your purpose on earth. Grant us the courage to champion the well-being of ourselves and our neighbors. Help us to embrace and respect difference, to shun idolatry, and to have balance in our lives. All thanks and praise! Amen.

Litany

LEADER: O give thanks to the Lord for the gift of family and community; for the ties that bind us to one another in sickness and health, in joy and sorrow, through the wilderness and mountaintop. We stand in gratitude.

PEOPLE: **In gratitude, gracious Savior, we celebrate the power and strength of family and community, the bloodlines that run deep; that reflect the link to the original goodness with which you anointed all creation at the beginning of time.**

LEADER: We honor the goodness born of love and relationships; symbolized in the ideal of family and unity. We recognize the oneness of blood that yokes us as family and that joins us as the Body of Christ. In Christ's Body, we share the blood of the cup of the New Testament.

PEOPLE: **We are all one at the table banquet prepared for us by Jesus of Nazareth, where we drink the cup and eat the bread. May we be one at all the tables where we come together and eat. May we honor oneness and respect individuality.**

LEADER: We celebrate families and extended families. We thank God for putting extended families in our lives that love and care for us because they want to.

PEOPLE: May human togetherness always be a cause to celebrate. Help us, merciful God, to be like Jesus as he cared for and taught his disciples; let us band together as we celebrate this [*homecoming or reunion*]. Let us all be blessed. Bless our home communities; grant those who could not be with us, peace and contentment. Protect us and our extended families as we return. Let the spirit of the [*reunion or homecoming*] dwell with us until we meet again.

ALL: Praise God for all expressions of healthy, loving families. In thanksgiving, as we stand on the brink of this new day, on the horizon of hope, framed by a mustard seed of faith—let the bonds honored here transcend time in the love of Christ Jesus.

Vow of Commitment

O Divine Redeemer, creator of family and community: we humbly bow before you, as part of your good and noble creation. Out of your mouth, you spoke the word and we became living creatures. We thank you for the presence of relationships in our lives. In joyful celebration, we vow to do all we can to spread harmony all around. We pledge ourselves, individually and collectively, toward honoring your rule over us. Gracious peacemaker, we desire to let your light shine through us wherever we go. Through your merciful kindness and grace, we can be shepherds to your flocks, we can mold wonderful relationships and loving families.

Benevolent One, we can be a "balm in Gilead" for those we meet on this Christian journey; we can help "make the wounded whole." Help us point them to you, Lord, as the "wheel in the middle of the wheel," when our families or organizations need to move forward; as "Jacob's ladder" when your children need to "climb higher, higher." Precious

Lord, we can all sit with you at the "welcome table" when we need justice and right behavior, even when family and community problems arise or when someone has erred or betrayed a trust.

So blessed by your love, we can sit as neighbors; we can "go tell it on the mountains, over the hills and everywhere," what Jesus has done for us. We lift our voices and sing about our commitment and our openness to you, gracious Lord, to our neighbors and ourselves in a communion of love.

Suggested Colors

Red and green are the colors for homecoming and family reunions. Red stands for love, living blood, emotion, ardor, strife, anger, passion, and warmth. Green symbolizes life, love, freshness, growth, perspective, healing, peace, visibility, and the divine.

Scriptures

Let [us] hear of your steadfast love in the morning, for in you [we] put my [our] trust. (Ps. 143:8)

As for me and my household, we will serve the LORD. (Josh. 24:15b)

[Jesus] said to them, "Where is your faith?" They were afraid and amazed, and said to one another, "Who then is this, that he commands even the winds and the water, and they obey him?" (Luke 8:25)

And hope does not disappoint us, because God's love has been poured into our hearts through the Holy Spirit that has been given to us. (Rom. 5:5)

Poem of Reflection

FAMILY TIES AND REUNION JOYS

Mama and Daddy,
Granny and Gramps,
Sister, brother, uncle, aunt and cousins galore:
Lil' Sis, Big Sis, Joe-Boy, Junior
Nana, Nannie, Unkie—
Husband, wife, honey, sugar:
Words of endearment,
Words of honor,
Words of relation.
All God's people,
Kin and others
By blood, selection, ordination, and choice.

God gives people choice:
Freedom to love, to grow,
Freedom to do right and wrong.
How blessed are we.
Families exist and love,
Have a heritage to pass on.
Pictures, quilts, Bibles, memories
Joys, sorrows, hopes.

Can we learn to love?
Can we learn to forgive?
Can we embody the beauty and hurt of our past,
Embrace the present,
And have a world for the future?
Can we be a family and survive?
Can we trust God enough?

MOTHER'S DAY

Occasion

Mothers are loving, female parents—some by giving birth, others through adoption and caring. Today we join others throughout the world as we honor mothers' love. In the Bible, God is a mother to Israel and to the world. God is symbolized in ways we experience mothering: as a wet nurse, seamstress, mother hen, mother eagle. We are mothered and held in the Lord's bosom, where we experience nurture and care.

Mary was the mother of Jesus. Anna Julia Cooper was a mother of Pan-African scholarship and Black education. Clara Hale was the mother for numerous addicted and abandoned babies. Catherine Dunham is a mother of African American choreography, anthropology, and dance. Mahalia Jackson was a mother of gospel music. Harriet Tubman and

Sojourner Truth were mothers to runaway slaves. Fannie Lou Hamer and Rosa Parks, along with countless unnamed others, are mothers for the 1960s Civil Rights movement. [*Selected names*] are mothers in our own community and church. Motherhood is a ministry.

We honor the ministry of mothers. Mothers are special. They guide and lead us. Mothers of the church are noble persons of authority and understanding. We look to them for wisdom and spiritual teaching. Mothers have offered hundreds of intercessory prayers, soothed thousands of fevers, made or selected countless Easter outfits, and baked or bought dozens of cookies for vacation Bible school.

Mothers have passed on folk wisdom, given advice, learned when to keep silent, and helped rear grandchildren. Mothers are women who wear many hats: spouse, parent, friend, sister, grandmother, and aunt. Mothers who love the Lord and walk by faith. Today we thank God for all mothers and celebrate their true spirit of love, nurture, compassion, leadership, patience, creativity, and joy. We challenge mothers to see their role as ordained by God, and as an opportunity to choose, to know balance, and to be guided by prayer.

Welcome

Greetings in the name of Christ Jesus! We, the members of [*church name*], deem it a privilege to welcome each of you to our Mother's Day celebration. We lift our voices, making a joyful noise unto the Lord in thanksgiving for mothers everywhere. We cherish the courage, fortitude, and insight of mothers, evident when they have made a way out of no way.

This day we honor the women who gave us birth and nonbiological mothers who daily nurture and pray for us. On behalf of the pastor, officers, and members of [*church name*], we welcome you. As we welcome each of you, we invite you to think on several things.

Think of the gift of life mothers bring to us all. Think of those adoptive, biological, extended family, and foster-care mothers who teach us our prayers, wipe dirty noses, help

our energies to be a part of extended families, thanking God that we do not have to rear our children alone as the church obeys the call to create family in service to the gospel. We celebrate the birth of children, ideas, and movements. We bless the bonding of mother to child. We anticipate and welcome mothers-to-be, as they anticipate the birth or placement of little ones in their homes and hearts. We respect those women who choose not to have children of their own but who support the children of others. We bless those women who desire children, but are unable to give birth, and yet give love to the child in all of us. We honor the many expressions of motherhood as a glimmer of God's grace. Amen.

Suggested Colors

Yellow and orange are the colors for Mother's Day. Yellow suggests liveliness, animation, radiance, good cheer, wisdom, knowledge, intelligence, inspiration, and a reflection of God's glory. Orange symbolizes the earth, autumn, warmth, fruitfulness, cheerfulness, and richness.

Scriptures

For it was you who formed my inward parts; you knit me together in my mother's womb. I praise you, for I am fearfully and wonderfully made. Wonderful are your works; that I know very well. (Ps. 139:13-14)

Then justice will dwell in the wilderness, and righteousness abide in the fruitful field. The effect of righteousness will be peace, and the result of righteousness, quietness and trust forever. (Isa. 32:16-17)

When [Jesus] saw their faith, he said, "Friend, your sins are forgiven you." (Luke 5:20)

And this is my prayer, that your love may overflow more and more with knowledge and full insight to help you to determine what is best. (Phil. 1:9-10a)

Poem of Reflection

MOTHERS: ELEGANT WARRIORS, FEARLESS HEROES

Mothers fight for their children, their mates
Sometimes (not often enough) for themselves.
Mothers know no fear when it comes to kin,
Especially those babies they call their own.
Mothers would rather die
Than lose those babies they carried
In reality and hope in their hearts.

This bond is so strong
The pain is so long:
Of the difficulties amid the joy
Of the maturing and of the love
Of mother and child.

Mothers love and care;
Mothers invent, do magical things, make us smile
Mothers make the best hot chocolate on wintry days
Mothers make the best care packages, the best meals
Mothers make that special ingredient that can't be packaged
Mothers add love and their knowledge of us.
When they send things on the bus
To us college students
Who're trying to be grown
But haven't gotten there yet.

Who are mothers?
Are they the image we have of them?
Are they only cooks and bottle washers?
Are they decision makers and earth shakers?

Mothers need love and respect,
A bit of thanks
A hug, some care,
Just for being themselves
Bearing the weight of the world:
Mothers are God's extraordinary gift to the world.

FATHER'S DAY

Occasion

Blessings and glory to God and congratulations to all fathers. Fathers, our male parents, come in all shapes and forms, with many desires, dreams, avocations, and abilities. Today we join people throughout the world as we sacredly reflect on the ministry of fatherhood. Today we celebrate the many fathers in our lives: biological, adopted, extended family, and mentors.

The Bible tells the stories of many fathers and their struggles to be good parents as part of God's call on their lives. Abraham, Isaac, Jacob, Joseph, Moses, Samuel, Saul, and David wrestled with being a father to their immediate family and to the nation of Israel. Jesus speaks of God as *Abba*, to denote an intimate, deeply felt relationship of responsibility and love.

Many African American men have been fathers for the greater good of human dignity. George Washington Carver and Charles Drew were fathers of science. Nat Turner and Denmark Vesey were fathers of protest against injustice. Samuel Cornish and John Russwurm were fathers of journalism. Carter G. Woodson was the father of Black history. James Weldon Johnson was one of the fathers of the National Association for the Advancement of Colored People (NAACP). [*Names of local fathers*] are fathers in our community and in our church.

We honor fathers as we thank God for all fathers and celebrate the true spirit of love, nurture, compassion, strength, vision, and provision expressed by fathers. Fathers are spouses, parents, brothers, and grandfathers who have loved the Lord and walked in grace through faith. We look to them for unconditional love, guidance, and determination. We prayerfully challenge fathers to see their place of ministry as a God-given blessing and noble responsibility.

Welcome

Glory and honor to God, and blessings in the name of Christ Jesus. The pastor, officers, and members of [*name of church*] welcome you in joy as we participate in our [*number*] annual Father's Day program. We welcome you to join with us in honoring the nobility, elegance, and demands of being a father. Think of the responsibility fathers bear in the realm of being leaders, providers, and nurturers. Think of the adoptive, foster-care, and extended family fathers. Think of the fathers who provide spiritual, financial, and emotional support to countless children.

We welcome and invite you to recognize the fathers of the church, the African American fathers of history who have had dreams, have offered intercessory prayers, have guided us, encouraged us, loved us, taught us to be strong, to use our imagination and improve ourselves and our communities. We thank God for fathers. We are grateful for fathers who know Jesus and realize that God's grace, full of mercy and justice, is the force that gives all of us life and the opportunity to be fathers. We welcome you to reflect on your own fathers and perhaps on your role as a father. We welcome you to be at home with us and to let us take care of you. We welcome you to visit at any time. Welcome, welcome. In the name of Jesus, welcome.

Prayer

O gracious God of all creation, God of fathers since the beginning of time and today: we bless you and thank you for ordaining men to be fathers in our lives. How grateful are we for the life made possible with the support of these men. Dear Lord, you father those who have no father. Wonderful Creator, your relationship with all the world teaches us how to father, how to love—a love shaped by justice, mercy, and discipline. As Father, you hold us when we are weak; guide us through life's storms; provide for us and love us unconditionally, when others do not want to and when we cannot love ourselves.

O God, bless all fathers with the gifts of wisdom, knowledge, love, compassion, and the ability to be a good listener to their spouses, children, to themselves. Let fathers find favor with you and help them bring their families closer to you. Help fathers discipline out of love, not out of anger. Help them be forgiving and not judgmental. Give fathers the courage to seek necessary counsel for their problems. Help fathers to know that men, too, have feelings, hurt, and do not need to have all the answers to all life's problems. Dear Shepherd, help fathers to anchor their hope and strength in you, not in the things they do, say, or have. Help us to love and respect our fathers in their ministry of fatherhood. Help families be partnerships between all parents and their children with strong church and community support. All blessings and honor are yours, dear God. Amen.

Litany

LEADER: Today we observe the ministry of fatherhood as an honorable commitment to God and God's people.

PEOPLE: **Thank you, precious Savior, Creator and model of fatherhood, for ordaining this relationship.**

LEADER: We honor and salute these fathers, living and dead, who have given love and support to the children of the world.

PEOPLE: **We rejoice, blessed Shepherd, for this service and for those we honor. Let us love and respect fathers worldwide.**

LEADER: Help fathers to overcome disappointment, hardship, and discrimination. Teach us, blessed Jesus, to be fathers who are sensitive to our family needs: to love and be loved, to be strong and gentle, faithful and true.

PEOPLE: **O ever-present Emmanuel, help us to know, respect, and love our fathers. Help all fathers to love and respect the boundaries of their children, to be a friend, parent, and source of inspiration.**

ALL: **May God bless us, as parent and child, to be part of the community of faith, to love others and ourselves as part of God's beautiful creation; honoring fathers and fathers honoring us.**

Vow of Commitment

O Rose of Sharon, O Bright and Morning Star: Father of Moses and Mandela, Father of the [*church name family*]. We thank you for the privilege and joy of fatherhood. We recommit our lives as sacred gifts ordained by God to lead and to love. Help us to be beacons to the world, help us to be part of the solution and not the problem. Empower us to receive your anointing and to be in relationships of equality and joy. Give us the strength to be fathers, to be present and inspiring for our children. In response to these gifts, we pledge our trust.

We welcome the opportunity of the ministry of fatherhood—to walk with God and lead all children. We commit ourselves to foster extended families, thanking God that we can help rear our children and those of our neighbors. Help us to act as a church family called by God and the gospel to serve. We know and accept our responsibility to help support our families: spiritually, mentally, emotionally, financially. We celebrate newness, life, and growth. We bless the relationships of fathers and children. We pray for fathers-to-be. We pray for those men who have chosen not to be fathers, but who serve as leaders and role models by all they say and do. We vow to be open to what God wants to do with our lives. We salute fathers that they may live in dignity and love throughout the world as expressions of God's hope and love.

Suggested Colors

Blue and red are the colors for Father's Day. Blue suggests serenity, peace, space, work, calm, royalty, and tends to be a unifying element. Red depicts living blood, life, grandeur, love, courage, and passion.

Scripture

I will sing of your steadfast love, O Lord, forever; with my mouth I will proclaim your faithfulness to all generations. (Ps. 89:1)

Listen, children, to a father's instruction, and be attentive, that you may gain insight. (Prov. 4:1)

"No one can serve two masters; for a slave will either hate the one and love the other, or be devoted to the one and despise the other. You cannot serve God and wealth." (Matt. 6:24)

Now we have received not the spirit of the world, but the Spirit that is from God, so that we may understand the gifts bestowed on us by God. (1 Cor. 2:12)

Poem of Reflection

FATHERS: NOBLE, GENTLE SPIRITS

Fathers are noble and strong
Full of courage, full of feelings.
We forget fathers have pain
We expect them to have all the answers;
Yet, fathers are not God,
Only God can be God.

Do we expect too much of fathers?
Do we expect too little?
Do we train little boys to be fathers?
Do we expect them to know how to father
As soon as little boys have children?

We must train fathers to be fathers
Love them when they're still under construction;
Love them when they are grand.
They are our heroes,
And loved us into adulthood,
But who are fathers, anyway?

Fathers are gentle spirits,
Boys grown into men,
Yet clinging to their toys.
Fathers pass on the greater joys of life;
Fathers give their families and friends
The great dreams they imagine,
Their faith in the Lord.
The Lord is the author and finisher of their faith,
The Lord makes a way for them out of no way.

Who are our fathers?
Male parents,
Friends and husbands,
With needs, wants, desires.
Fathers need and give love.
A father is a special gift from God.

WOMEN'S DAY

Occasion

Today, we celebrate the [*number*] annual Women's Day celebration of [*name of the church*]. Women's Day is a special event in our church's life. This day brings our church family and guests together to help us fulfill our Christian mission and outreach. The women of [*church name*] form a cloud of witnesses to the world about what Jesus has done and is doing for us. We follow the models of Prophet Deborah, Queen Esther, and Mother Hagar, as we lead this congregation in praise and stewardship. Today we celebrate ourselves.

We salute the women of [*church name*] of [*city, state*] as we press on in Christ Jesus to the mark of higher calling (Phil. 3:14). Through God's grace and in faith, we stand tall with other women, men, and children—united in love to do God's work. We share in taking care of our community, we support the total nurture, love, and maturity in the Lord in our neighbors. As Marian Anderson sang and Jurena Lee preached, as Mary McCleod Bethune taught, as Shirley Chisholm legislated, we sing, preach, and teach love, truth, and peace in all that we do. We stand united in Christ Jesus. Praise be!

Welcome

To the pastor, other distinguished pulpit guests, officers and members of the [church name] church family, sisters and brothers in Christ Jesus:

An invitation to meet in God's house is always a blessed time. We have come to praise God, to celebrate our community, and to celebrate being women. God created males and females and all created order as good. God created us in the divine image of love. We welcome you to celebrate our divine goodness in song, scripture, and the preached Word. The doors to the church, to the Body of Christ are always open. If there is anything we can do to make you feel more loved and cared for, please let us know. We are here to serve.

We, the women of [church name] stand together in the name of Christ Jesus and welcome you. We stand in the tradition of abolitionist Sojourner Truth; Underground Railroad conductor Harriet Tubman; and Civil Rights activist Fannie Lou Hamer, to lead our people to affirm all: men, women, and children in the quest to love and be loved. Join us in this sanctified journey of freedom and wholeness. We welcome you to our church home, we welcome you to celebrate our life in Christ Jesus. We welcome you to this program. May you be refreshed and renewed. Be well. Be welcomed.

Prayer

Gracious God, Creator of all, the one who always loves us; we come today in celebrating creation. We praise your mighty name! We honor you and bless you, dear one, great physician. We give you thanks, for we know just as you guard and tend to the sparrow, to the lilies of the field, we know that you care for us.

God, we thank you for your loving-kindness, justice, and mercy. We thank you for this day as the women of [*church name*] stand united as a living testimony to the world of what the Lord has done and is doing through us.

Lord God, Lamb of God, who brings life to us, empower us to walk the walk of righteousness and talk the talk of Christian unity. Let this Women's Day program be successful in all ways. Let our hearts and minds be open to hear what you would have us hear; help our facial expressions and voices reflect loving strength and nurturing power. Let us be teachers, good stewards, and creative servants with all our gifts. We pray as Hannah, Samuel's mother, and as Mary in her Magnificat for your anointing to live a blessed and sacred life, O God. In your Son's name, through the power of the Holy Spirit. Amen.

Litany

LEADER: We arise dear God, as women of courage, to do your will, to do justice, walk humbly, and befriend our neighbors.

PEOPLE: **With courage, Lord, we accept your invitation to be just, strong, and willing to befriend women, men, and children everywhere.**

LEADER: We stand tall, El Olam, God everlasting, as did opera singer Marian Anderson, against the shortsightedness of the Daughters of the American Revolution, to use her God-given talents to lift up your name and the name of her people.

PEOPLE: **Like Marian, we sing your name, every day and every hour; we celebrate who we are and whose we are.**

LEADER: We persevere, overcoming the oppression of society and self, as did Mae Jemison, our first African American female astronaut, to circle the earth and do experiments on her space mission.

PEOPLE: **Through grace we leap over oppression from the outside. We pray for the strength to overcome the self-inflicted oppression that may be hidden from us.**

LEADER: We unite as women; overcoming petty disagreements and personal choices to serve the community and to serve ourselves. We climb the ladders of sin, jealousy, fear, denial, lack, and unbelief to reach the hilltops of health and wholeness.

PEOPLE: **With you, loving God, we can move mountains; we are made whole. The storms of illness, disease, and bad feelings cannot obstruct the power of your Spirit on us to worship you, to serve the present age, to maintain our families, to love every mother's child, and to be loved.**

LEADER: Blessed are you, O God! Blessed are we who desire righteousness! Blessed are those who need you and have not yet experienced your power. Blessed are the women who listened to what Jesus said as he showed us living love—those who stood at the foot of the cross, prepared Jesus' body for burial, went to the empty tomb, and witnessed the resurrection.

ALL: **We now go and tell the world about Jesus and about how we are blessed. Jesus is come, the Comforter is One.**

In him, we find rest. We Christian women are up to the test! Blessed be!

Vow of Commitment

On this sacred day, we rededicate our lives to Christ and the well-being of the church, the Body of Christ. We take seriously the vows made by us or on our behalf at our baptism. We pledge our loyalty to the church—to the members of [church name]. We promise to:

- support the proclamation of God's Word, read scripture daily, listen attentively to the message, share a gospel word, live our lives by the Word
- minister to all members: female and male, the sick and the well, learned and unlearned, rich and poor, young, middle-age, and old
- partake of communion, celebrate the reconciling love of God demonstrated in the sharing of the bread and the cup, celebrate the spirit of this meal in all we say and do in the church community and in the larger world community
- be who God has blessed women to be, to practice a ministry that names that which is right and names all violence
- practice a ministry of self-esteem, renewal, and reconciliation

We take the charge to be Christlike, to stand boldly for the Lord, to disciple others in love. We avoid violence, from physical abuse to the verbal abuse of gossip, which violates the character of others.

We stand before God and the church and we pledge our commitment as women of the Lord, to be strong, proud, smart, loving, giving, caring, leading persons. We will only allow those into our lives who have the room to let us be who God created us to be.

Suggested Colors

Pink and black are the colors for Women's Day. Pink (rose, fuchsia, or hot pink) denotes warmth, welcome, passion, high spirits. Black symbolizes solidarity, strength, power, infinity.

Scriptures

This is the day that the LORD has made; let us rejoice and be glad in it. (Ps. 118:24)

And hope does not disappoint us, because God's love has been poured into our hearts through the Holy Spirit that has been given to us. (Rom. 5:5)

As for me, I would seek God, and to God I would commit my cause. (Job 5:8)

"Whatever you ask for in prayer with faith, you will receive." (Matt. 21:22)

Poem of Reflection

WOMEN ANCHORED IN CHRIST JESUS

We sing the word, Woman!
That's who we are:
Strong, black, beautiful, bold,
Warm, blessed, faithful.

There are times when the world must know:
We are more than sister, wife, and mother,
Chief cook, maid, and dirty diaper changer;
We are happy, sad, joyous, angry, soulful, brilliant,
Aggressive, soft, passive, energetic, imaginative, elaborate, plain:
Women are God's created.

We are made in God's image:
Creative, loving, talkative yet quiet.
We need to love and to be loved;
We require respect,
We have dreams,
We need room in our lives
To be who we are.

We, daughters of God, are strong and well and whole.
We live the sacred life:
We grow, think, run, do, make, shout, dance, be,
Scale mountains, plant gardens, travel oceans,
Have children, not have children,
Teach and learn, pray and do ministry.
Live as Christian women,
With Jesus as our friend and guide;
Knowing that all things are possible.

We love ourselves well.
Proud that God loves us just as we are.
Proud, happy, scared, mischievous, loving women,
Regal in our color purple,
God's chosen in the world.

MEN'S DAY

Occasion

To the pastor, officers, pulpit dignitaries, members and visitors of [*church name*]: It is celebration time in the life of our church. Today is Men's Day. We come in the name of Jesus, empowered by the Holy Spirit, to lift up the Christian life and to offer thanksgiving for the opportunity to be Christian fathers, husbands, brothers, and friends. We celebrate being created in God's image. We celebrate our partnership with all men and women, especially with those who claim an allegiance to God as revealed in Christ Jesus.

We stand victorious for the Lord; our songs lift up Zion; our prayers tell of God's goodness and mercy to us. We remember the wisdom of Solomon, the repentance of David, the courage of Joseph, the love and care of Simon of Cyrene, the zeal of Paul, and the ministry of Samuel. We stand tall and proud in the Lord's name. We salute the men of [church name], of [city, state], of the world as we grow in love, gentleness, strength, courage, and grace. We join with our faith community to raise our children, to be true to ourselves, to stand for justice and freedom, to be helpful in all our relationships, to do all that we do to God's glory.

As [name of one of your church's founders] ministered, as Martin Luther King, Jr. taught and preached, as Malcolm X transformed, as Marcus Garvey led, as Adam Clayton Powell, Jr. preached and legislated, we celebrate change, knowledge, and leadership in all we do today. Hallelujah!

Welcome

To the pastor, officers, members, and friends of [church name]: It is good, so good to gather together to glorify God! The Lord has blessed the men of this church to love and serve the Lord and the Body of Christ. We celebrate our call to stewardship of our time, talents, and finances. We celebrate that God created everything good, and created us in divine goodness. We welcome you to our Christ-filled home; we welcome you as a member of the family of God, to join us in praise and prayer.

How good it is to come together! The psalmist tells us to praise with psaltery, harp, and dance, with trumpets, stringed instruments, and resounding cymbals. Here in God's sanctuary, let everything that has breath praise the Lord! (Ps. 150).

We, the men of [church name], welcome you in the name of Jesus. We delight in sharing our skills and gifts in this service and in our lives like other African men who have gone before: church leader, St. Augustine of Hippo (North Africa), educator and Masonic founder, Prince Hall, and scientist and inventor, Benjamin Banneker. We welcome you to join us to serve the Lord and commit our lives to the good of the church, our community, our people. We welcome you here. Know that you have a home with us. The doors of this church are always open to you. Welcome.

Prayer

Gracious God, Everlasting Lord and Creator, we thank you for being you, and we bless your holy name. Lord, you have been our dwelling place for all generations. Your loving-kindness and mercy sustained our foreparents on slave cargo ships, in the fields, at the birth of our children, at the death of our parents, at the marriages and life-changing experiences of our loved ones. Lord, we thank you. We thank you for sustaining us and for giving us an opportunity to come together on the [*number*] annual Men's Day.

Lord, empower and anoint our program today. Let the blessings shared here go with us as we leave this hallowed place. O Ancient of Days, help us to share your love. Bless the participants and gathered congregation. Help us to lift our voices in word and song that brings us together. We unite our hearts in affirming your presence in worship and our commitment to one another.

Please transform burdens into blessings. Bless those who suffer, especially those young Black men and women incarcerated in our prison systems. Lord, show us how to minister to them and how to love our young boys and girls enough so that they may know joy, love, and self-esteem in a way that they will never end up in jail. Help our daughters and our sons to love themselves. Show us how to be our neighbor's keeper, loving without crippling, without trying to fix others and without trying to play God.

Help us to be good stewards with all finances raised today. Let the joy and love shared today inspire all of those gathered. Blessings, honor, and glory, gracious Creator. Amen.

Litany

LEADER: We stand, O God, as men of love, to honor, love, and obey you. We place before you our concerns of freedom and justice for all people.

PEOPLE: **With love, O Redeemer, we stand on your promises of salvation and mercy, as we respond in thanksgiving—committed to the growth and nurture of ourselves and our families; to the well-being of your church and the integrity of your call on our lives.**

LEADER: We rejoice at the call of lay ministries wherever we are. We stand for the liberation of all people in the heritage of Frederick Douglass. We are open to be a prophetic voice like that of W. E. B. DuBois.

PEOPLE: **Like Douglass and DuBois, we call for revolutionary change in our own hearts; to be neither master nor slave, but truly free to be who God created us to be.**

LEADER: We lift our voices with the power and elegance of singer Paul Robeson, and we claim our rich heritage and our African heritage in the spirit of writer Alex Haley.

PEOPLE: **O great God, how richly you have blessed us! With hope and desire we take the authority to speak boldly in the Lord with talent and confidence.**

LEADER: We speak in gratitude for the past, rejoice in the present, and anticipate the future that we nurture today with our commitment to be Christian leaders, parents, partners, children, and friends, in love and unity.

PEOPLE: **Together we stand, as the Body of Christ, none superior or inferior, all on a pilgrimage toward divine love; called to proclaim the gospel, the good news.**

ALL: **Together we praise you, O Lord! In honor of Men's Day, we thank you. Blessed be you, O God. Blessed be** all your children. Help us to hold to the strength of Jesus, to stand in the faith of the early church and in the joy and holiness of the saints. Exaltations and joy! Amen.

Vow of Commitment

On this sacred day, we pledge ourselves anew to the worship and service of God and for the love of the church, on a daily basis. We hold dear our commitment to be Christ-like and honor our baptismal vows. We celebrate the liberating value and holiness we experience at the Lord's Supper. We stand in humble joy:

• To be witnesses of the power of Christ Jesus in our lives to others and to encourage their well-being and spiritual growth
• To serve all members and all people regardless of race, creed, gender, class—as Jesus served during his ministry on earth
• To support sharing the gospel by listening to and living by the preached and written Word
• To participate in the rituals and rules of the church; to be a part of the teaching and learning witness of the church; to tithe; to give of our time, talents, and finances as God has so blessed us
• To be who God has blessed us and called us to be; to practice God's ministry of forgiving

We take the call to be like Jesus, in season and out of season; to disciple others in love. We look to the Lord for spiritual strength and for the ability to abstain from physical, mental, emotional, or spiritual acts of fleshly violence and abuse. We pledge to let the Lord God guide every aspect of our lives that we might truly be ambassadors for Christ, for God's living, redeeming, reconciling love.

Suggested Colors

Green and blue are the suggested colors for Men's Day. Green denotes steadiness, thoughtfulness, freshness, healing, peace, visibility, growth, and the divine. Blue denotes serenity, space, coolness, work, peacemaking, and unity.

Scriptures

Happy are those who make the LORD *their trust, who do not turn to the proud, to those who go astray after false gods.* (Ps. 40:4)

For you shall worship no other god, because the LORD, *whose name is Jealous, is a jealous God.* (Exod. 34:14)

"This is my commandment, that you love one another as I have loved you. No one has greater love than this, to lay down one's life for one's friends." (John 15:12-13)

My brothers and sisters, whenever you face trials of any kind, consider it nothing but joy, because you know that the testing of your faith produces endurance; and let endurance have its full effect, so that you may be mature and complete, lacking in nothing. (James 1:2-4)

Poem of Reflection

MEN: LOVERS OF THE LORD

Men stand with the Lord,
The foundation of the Creator and Maker of all.
We are strong and weak, rich and poor;
Do not define us by what we do and who we know;
We belong to God.

We love the Lord and our families,
We plant and build and play.
We are strong:
Even when we hurt so bad that if we cried out in pain
All creation would groan;
The earth would tremble and shake—
We hold our pain in—and pretend it's not there.

Don't let our masks make you think
we don't care:
We care, we care deeply.

We're proud of our fathers, natural and adopted
We honor and respect our mothers at home and afar,
Our sisters and brothers are closer than many,
Our friends share our growing pains and make us laugh.
Our wives and partners share a bond with us,
An intimacy with us and God.
Our children are our seed, the essence of our love.
We are ourselves, noble and free,
Bold warriors, gentle guides,
Searching for our destiny.

We remember our history:
We inherit the evils of slavery and racism;
We remember the times we've been 'buked and scorned;
The times our parents were humiliated.
We remember that Jesus truly loves us.

We know that men can stand tall, love, organize,
Create, be somebody, do good,
We are already somebody,
With God's grace we can save our churches, our communities,
Our boys, our girls,
Ourselves.

PASTOR'S APPRECIATION DAY

Occasion

From the times of Abraham to Esther, Jesus and Paul to Phoebe and Priscilla, from Sojourner Truth and Frederick Douglass to our own [*name of pastor and name of spouse, if married*], men and women have accepted God's call on their lives to serve, nurture, and guide faithful believers. These persons study, teach, and preach God's Word, visit the sick and troubled, marry the beloved, baptize those new in the faith, consecrate and serve the Lord's Supper or Eucharist, counsel the concerned, bury the dead, work for justice and freedom for the oppressed, head building projects, press for outreach and discipleship, and serve as CEO with Christ as the Head, with the support of the congregation. Today we honor our pastor.

We praise God, in humility, for the opportunity to live and to serve. We acknowledge the blessedness of life and the assurance we have in God for the wonderful grace and redemptive love that allows us to serve. Today we honor our pastor [*and spouse*] for [*his, or her, or their*] commitment to God, to the [*name of church*] family and to the world. In a spirit of thanksgiving, we honor the one(s) who has [*have*] served us this year. As we celebrate today, let us embrace a hopeful imagination and a loving spirit that we, as pastor and church, may live and teach the good news of Christ Jesus.

Welcome

To the pastor [*and spouse*], officers, members of [*church name*], the [*name of city*] community, visitors, friends: We greet you in our Lord's most precious name on the occasion of our pastor's appreciation. Today we honor our pastor [*and wife or husband*]. We celebrate [*his, her, or their*] gifts and the impact [*he, she, or they*] have had and are having on this body and our larger community. We stand before God and you, with grateful hearts and hopeful anticipation that everyone will here receive blessings and inspiration in this service.

Our leaders are our guides. They inspire us to be open to God's will in our lives, for we all have a ministry. God created each of us and has anointed each of us with unique talents and special ways of participating in God's world. Each of us, as members of the church, are to minister in our daily lives to our families, friends, and neighbors. We welcome you today to celebrate God's call on all our lives as we remember [*names of pastor and spouse*] with special prayers, offerings, and love.

We praise and thank God for ordained and lay ministers. We welcome the challenges that our sacred life in Christ opens to us. We invite each of you to rejoice in the Lord, give thanks and praise in all we say and do! We welcome you to join us in praising God, honoring our pastor, and celebrating the office of ministry.

Prayer

Glorious Redeemer and Divine Spirit: We praise your name, your everlasting grace. Your bounty is marvelous, your love for creation, untiring. It is this love that sustains us and has given us the vision of the church and church leadership. We celebrate, O God, your gift of pastoral service to the church. We thank you for pastors and chaplains, who serve in churches, hospitals, and other institutions throughout the world.

We ask special grace for our pastor, [names] and [his or her] family, their lives and their ministry. Give them serenity and joy in their walk, wisdom and knowledge in their goals, and clarity and discernment in their life's challenges. O Lord, as a church, help us to be Christlike to our pastor, church staff, and to one another. Help us to work together to bring your Word to those who are dying of spiritual malnutrition. Gracious Creator, be the rock, shield, comforter, and teacher for [name of pastor]. Give [him or her] a sense of humor, and the strength to stand against powers and principalities, to preach in season and out of season, to have the courage to use fully [her or his] divinely given gifts.

Help us to love [pastor's name] and appreciate [his or her] divine call and human frailty. We honor and praise your holiness and grace, O God. Amen.

Litany

LEADER: O God, you call us to lead and guide. You call men and women to be shepherds to your beloved children.

PEOPLE: **Bless your servants with an ability to see, hear, and do your will in gratitude and humility for the spiritual well-being of the church community.**

LEADER: As we embrace God's call on our lives, we desire courage to do the impossible, insight to dream the mysterious, love to forgive the unforgivable, and the willingness to see all humanity and ourselves as redeemable through Christ Jesus.

PEOPLE: With open, receiving hearts we salute the ordained relationships between God, our pastor, and our [*church name*] family. We celebrate this ministry of [*number*] years. We bless and challenge this ministry toward increased heights of holiness and a zeal to catch on fire with the Holy Spirit.

ALL: **May we accept God's loving leadership as the model and means for being Christian followers and leaders committed to nonjudgmental love for our neighbors and for ourselves, that we may lead others in the walk of Christ.**

Vow of Commitment

O loving Creator God, you who fashioned creation out of nothing: we stand as pastor and members of [*church name*] on this blessed occasion to renew our vows to serve you. As father to the fatherless and mother to the motherless, we commit that we hear and do offer ourselves to serve this present age as guides, nurturers, parents, and friends to the wounded, the displaced, and the orphaned; to lead in showing the possibilities of transformation and reconciliation to the oppressed and the oppressor, to the battered and the batterer, to the learned and the unlearned, to rich and poor. For in God, there is no difference: neither male nor female, Jew nor Gentile, slave nor free (Gal. 3:28). Knowing that "the gifts and the calling of God are irrevocable," we submit our lives to your work (Rom. 11:28).

We recall our awe and excitement, our curiosity and our fear when we first realized your call on our lives. Your grace,

O God, has remained sufficient, despite our hesitation, mistakes, and weaknesses. We vow, O gracious Redeemer, to daily reflect your call on our lives in words, thoughts, and deeds. In faith through love, we pledge to study and share your Word; to stand in awe before you as we administer the sacraments, preach, teach, marry, bury, shepherd, love, and tend the flock of [church name].

Suggested Colors

Purple and red are the colors for Pastor's Appreciation Day. Purple symbolizes royalty , power, high energy, depth of feeling, and self-esteem. Red stands for love, living blood, emotion, ardor, strife, passion, anger, and warmth.

Scriptures

Set a guard over my mouth, O LORD; keep watch over the door of my lips. (Ps. 141:3)

I [the Lord] will give you shepherds [pastors] after my own heart, who will feed you with knowledge and understanding. (Jer. 3:15)

"And teaching them to obey everything that I [Jesus] have commanded you. And remember, I am with you always, to the end of the age." (Matt. 28:20)

For everything created by God is good, and nothing is to be rejected, provided it is received with thanksgiving; for it is sanctified by God's word and by prayer. If you put these instructions before the brothers and sisters, you will be a good servant of Christ Jesus, nourished on words of the faith and of the sound teaching that you have followed. (1 Tim. 4:4-6)

Poem of Reflection

PASTOR, PREACHER, TEACHER

Pastor stands before the congregation
And proclaims, "Thus saith the Lord!"
Utters prayers, baptizes folk,
Marries and buries with the best;
Shouts and sings with a loud voice
At morning and evening time;
Called by God to bring the Word
Blessed be, blessed be.

We treasure our pastor for kind words, great sermons,
Marvelous information, insight and compassion,
knowledge and patience,
For being the person God created,
To bring us beyond Calvary,
To the Resurrection and the New Jerusalem.

O pastor, preacher, teacher,
We depend on you to bring the Word from on high
To lift God's praises up to the sky and back to us,
In God we do trust.

We seek God through you.
You're not God.
You're more than the various roles you perform,
You are God's chosen;
We commend your work
May you be blessed.
Be true to yourself and your call.
God loves you, and us, through you.

Let's honor each other;
Giving honor to God,
Love to our neighbor, and to ourselves;
Pastor, preacher, teacher,
You, too, are God's creature,
We love you,
God bless you;
Well done!

OFFICERS' REDEDICATION DAY

Occasion

Since the earliest moments of worship in the "bush arbors," in the woods or behind sheds, African American leaders have galvanized others to praise God and to work together for freedom and justice, for the well being of the Black community. Today we gather to remember past and present persons who have accepted God's call to be church leaders. These men and women have dug deeply and given mightily. These officers have attended hours of meetings to plan strategies for the spiritual, religious, sociopolitical, and financial affairs of [*name of church*] congregation.

Though our church community has had its ups and downs, the faithful leaders and members of this congregation have stood together amid the storms of life and the radiance of bright noonday. We salute the officers of all our

◊◊◊ **73**

boards and auxiliaries [or name particular board], for their hard work and service to [church name], and for their support of Christian witness here and throughout the [name of city] community. May today inspire them to continue their ministry of teamwork and mutual concern for the church of God.

Welcome

To the distinguished pastor, officers, members, friends, and guests of [church name]: I take much joy and honor in greeting you in the name of Jesus Christ this glorious day. We welcome each of you to our celebration of commitment, community, and friendship as we salute the officers of [church name or specific organization in church].

Officers make a mark within our church structure and the community. They are ambassadors for Christ everywhere they go. Thus with glad hearts, we honor their service and witness, and welcome and invite you to participate fully with us. We hope you are inspired to become leaders in your community, church, and home. Leadership demands perseverance, commitment, vision, faith, and a love of the Lord and of people. Today we welcome you to join us in recognizing and honoring the role of officers and the ministry of leadership. We all join together in praise of God in this holy sanctuary, with prayer, song, word, and deed. Receive now our welcome; receive now the Lord!

Prayer

O sovereign Lord, leader of all leaders, our Shepherd and Savior: we thank you on this wonderful morning for life, health, strength, for community building, and for leadership. We thank you, O God, O Ancient of Days, for the call on our lives, to be followers and leaders. We are grateful to follow in the traditions of prophets of long ago, who wrestled with the call, but still brought the message and did the deed. Lord, make us worthy of your mission and your desire for relationship between you and your created people. Help us to sense the urgency of life-giving activity that nurtures the body, mind, and spirit.

Please give us the willingness to lead as Jesus led: to answer difficult questions, to follow through when feeling downtrodden, to hold to our "impossible dream." Yet, let us realize that the grace of our Lord is sufficient; that "[we] can do all things through him who strengthens [us]" (Phil. 4:13). Lord, give us you vision for the church, for "without a vision, the people perish" (Prov. 29:18). Anoint us with your wisdom, strength, and love to lead your people through. Amen.

Litany

LEADER: Rejoice, O people of God, come with hearts open for service in this present age. Let us gird our leadership with love, and pray for patience and diligent change of our hearts and deeds toward being Christlike in our task as church officers.

PEOPLE: **Hallelujah! Lord God! We shout glad hosannas of humility as we partake of your vision and your call on our lives.**

LEADER: We champion Christlike love in our board meetings, in our planning, and in our activities. We urge the place of unity and cooperation in all our affairs and in our work with the larger church community.

PEOPLE: **Lord, help us to support the work of all church boards. Give us insight as to our role together as an institution as your living witness to the world.**

LEADER: How good it is that men and women, girls and boys can dwell together in the household of faith and participate in many different ministries. Praise God for the lay ministries of deacons or stewards or elders, deaconesses or stewardesses, presbytery, convention, choirs, ushers, teachers, lay leaders, ministers' spouses, Sunday school, mission work, liturgy, evangelism, outreach, tithes, benevolence, children, youth, young adult, scouting [*name other ministries specific to your church here*].

ALL: **We rejoice at the richness of our ministries, the unity and diversity that our organizations represent. We so desire to do your will and your work. We thank you, O God, for the challenge and gifts of opportunities to serve.**

Vow of Commitment

Merciful Lord, we come to renew our vows of commitment to serve as members of boards at [*church name*]. While we often boast of our accomplishments, we know, O Lord, that you are our source of creativity and strength. Today we affirm our willingness to grow and learn in wisdom and knowledge of you and of our tasks for the church. We pledge our willingness to improve in things spiritual and practical: to study your Word, to study the guidebook for our various boards, to love you and exercise love for our board members by being on time, listening attentively, attending meetings, and shouldering our own responsibility.

We agree to serve in elected and appointed offices to the best of our ability. We will share the responsibility of keeping our organizations alive and growing through prayer, study, and hard work. Help us to give others an opportunity to be officers. We give ourselves as Hannah gave Samuel, to your service, O Lord. Blessed be your name.

Suggested Colors

The colors for officers' rededication are black and white. Black symbolizes solidarity, strength, power, and infinity. White symbolizes light, birth, life's ironies, and radiance.

Scriptures

Say to God, "How awesome are your deeds! Because of your great power, your enemies cringe before you. All the earth worships you; they sing praises to you, sing praises to your name." (Ps. 66:3-4)

[Says the Lord], I will lead the blind by a road they do not know, by paths they have not known I will guide them. I will turn the darkness before them into light, the rough places into level ground. These are the things I will do, and I will not forsake them. (Isa. 42:16)

"Whoever is faithful in a very little is faithful also in much, and whoever is dishonest in a very little is dishonest also in much." (Luke 16:10)

For we have become partners of Christ, if only we hold our first confidence firm to the end. (Heb. 3:14)

Poem of Reflection

OFFICERS AND LEADERS: COMMITTED TO THE CAUSE

Elections, appointments
Create leaders and officers,
For the guidance of the church;
The dedicated,
Never leave us in a lurch;
For they are committed to Jesus,
And to God's rule on earth.

Hard-working and creative,
Take little and make much,
Call upon us to do our part;
They begin by setting the mark
Of our dreams and our goals,
Of our church on the corner,
Set apart to bring the good news.

Officers have a thankless job;
We call them when things go wrong;
Do we commend them when things go right?

Everyone has a load to bear;
As we march to Zion,
But none of us carry the Lion's share.
We must do our part,
Giving the message is an art
In a world where there is much despair,
We often forget to share the good news;
That Jesus Christ does care.

Attention officers and leaders:
We depend on you,
To take care of church business,
To share with us the renewing faith of our Lord.
Jesus loves us, this we know,
For the Bible tells us so!

BOARD AND
AUXILIARY DAY

Occasion

The church is the Body of Christ. That body has many parts. Organizations and boards come from members of the body. Today we honor the ministry of support and cooperation by celebrating the [*year*] anniversary of [*name of board or organization*]. The call of the church is to proclaim the Word of God, to serve one another and the world, to baptize into the faith, and serve the bread and the wine in love. The work of the church depends on grace and the smooth functioning of all its parts. The [*name of the organization*] is an integral part of [*name of the church*].

This organization has served this church and the community in many ways by [*list three to five activities*]:

We praise God for the past, present, and future work of [*name of organization*]. Service in the Lord is an act of nobility, love, and dignity. We come in joy and thanksgiving on this special occasion to remember this board's activities and to praise God for their presence and work. May we all stand in faith, ready to grow, prepared to serve.

Welcome

"I was glad when they said to me, 'Let us go to the house of the LORD!'" (Ps. 122:1). We the members of the [*name of organization*] of the [*name of the church*] eagerly welcome you to this most auspicious occasion. Our pastor, officers, and members share in bringing this greeting. We thank God that you have come to be with us this special day, and for blessing us with your presence. The [*name of board or organization*] plays a key part in the life of our church. We are committed to expressing our love and adoration of God through our support of the church, the Body of Christ.

We welcome you to our service to the [*name of the city*] community and to this church where we have [*select one: served or performed or prepared the sanctuary*], for the glory of God. Our activity supports the worship here at [*church name*] and at the [*select one or as many as appropriate: convention, district conference, annual conference, association levels*]. It is our honor to have you here. You are at home, for this is God's house where all are welcome. Be welcome, be blessed. Come join with us in praise, have your souls filled, and take something away from here today to edify God and comfort yourselves.

Prayer

O Lord, our help in ages past, our hope for years to come: we come with thankful hearts and abounding joy, praising your holy name. We praise you, O God with song, prayer, and the gospel. We celebrate the call you have on our lives as members of [name of organization]. Thank you for this ministry. Help us, dear teacher and comforter, to embrace the challenges of service out of love.

Help us to work together for the good of the church and the world. Teach us how to let go of hurt and disagreement. Remind us, dear Savior, that our task is to help build, not tear down; to give and graciously receive; to serve, not to be a star. Yet, give us the grace and generosity to acknowledge the spirit and work of ourselves and others. Guide the leaders and members of [name of the organization] in planning and carrying out our activities.

We receive the charge to love and serve in quiet dignity, to be Christlike to everyone we have the opportunity to serve. Thank you for this day of celebration and acknowledgment. Amen.

Litany

LEADER: We shout praise of adoration, O God, to you for the gift of service and the shared joy of the community formed by our organization.

PEOPLE: **Thank you, O God, for a time to praise, a time to study, a time to serve, and a time to do the work of our ministry.**

LEADER: God, we thank you for your redeeming grace that gives us the faith to be at one with you and to work with our organizations, even when we disagree, misunderstand, and make bad decisions.

PEOPLE: **Merciful Lord, we celebrate the gifts of love, humility, and the grace to change and cooperate.**

LEADER: How joyous to have a sisterhood and brotherhood of believers who place Christ at the head of their lives and see organizational services as a ministry of our precious Lord.

PEOPLE: **Hosanna for the anointing to be partners in the gospel of truth and righteousness as we serve and reap the joy of the work the [*name of organization*] does.**

ALL: **May God grant us the peace, courage, and wisdom to be inspired, challenged leaders and followers, that the work of our organization will glorify you and bring us in closer communion with you and one another.**

Vow of Commitment

O wonderful, merciful Comforter and Guide: we recommit ourselves to the purpose and goals of [*name of organization*] as we work to uphold the ministry of our Lord and Savior Jesus Christ. As we serve this church, we take blessed assurance in the call you have on our lives. Help us, Gentle Savior, as you daily look beyond our faults to our needs, to see the needs of others and ourselves. As you strengthen us, we pledge to work together for the good of one another, individually and collectively. Loving Creator, give us a new vision as a church and as an organization created for the well-being of the larger church body. Lord, we are open to you for your grace of cleansing reconciliation that wipes away not only the tears of sorrow, but also the stains of greed, selfishness, false pride, jealousy, bitterness, and prejudice.

We accept your visions of love and compassion as our pathway to unspeakable joy, trust, and compassion for those who still do not know you. As we continue to grow, we look toward the altar, leaving all our cares and hurts. Be our joy in all we do. Amen.

Suggested Colors

Orange and white are the colors for boards and organizations. Orange symbolizes the earth, autumn, warmth, fruitfulness, cheerfulness, and richness. White, a combination of the colors of the rainbow, symbolizes purity, peace, light, and illumination.

Scriptures

It is good to give thanks to the LORD, to sing praises to your name, O Most High; to declare your steadfast love in the morning, and your faithfulness by night. (Ps. 92:1-2)

Commit your work to the LORD, and your plans with be established. (Prov. 16:3)

"Ask, and it will be given you; search, and you will find; knock, and the door will be opened for you." (Matt. 7:7)

And may the Lord make you increase and abound in love for one another and for all. (1 Thess. 3:12a)

Poem of Reflection

HAND IN HAND, TOGETHER

We meet, we pray, we sing, we work,
In the Name of Jesus,
In the power of the Holy Spirit,
To spread the gospel message,
To shout to the world,
Who we are, who are we!
We are children of Jesus!
We're strivin' to be Christlike,
Tryin' to make heaven our home on earth.

Do we speak and act like Christ?
Do we listen and hear in our meetings:
Do we do unto others in our activities:
As we would have them do unto us?

In our home:
Do we treat each other and our guests like Jesus would treat us?
Do we wear our Christlike spirit only in church?

God calls all of us: Children, youth, young adults, adults,
At work and at play,
To love the Lord with all our heart;
To love our neighbors as ourselves!

What is love: Love is active caring and respect.
Love is listening, love is doing, love is sharing,
To, for, with others,
As if we were
Listening, doing, sharing
With Christ—
Hand in hand, creating a better day,
A peaceful, healthy world.
Together, today: Jesus invites us.
Do we accept Christ's call?

GROUNDBREAKING, CORNERSTONE LAYING, AND MORTGAGE BURNING

Occasion

Many landmarks occur in the life of the church. These events give us an opportunity to stop and offer additional thanks to God for all our blessings and for allowing us to serve the [*name of the city*] community for [*number*] years. Today we are exceedingly grateful and happy to be celebrating our [*mortgage burning or cornerstone laying or groundbreaking*] day.

For Mortgage Burning

[*Number*] years ago, under the leadership of [*pastor or former pastor's name*] along with the support of our wonderful officers, members, and friends of [*church name*], we secured the finances and [*built or remodeled*] this edifice and dedicated it to the glory of God. In prayerful obedience, we have worked, tithed, and supported the completion of the building project and have come in joy and contentment to this moment. We know that God's name is majestic over all, and we see God's creative work in the heavens, the waters, and the earth. God has given humanity dignity of existence with great possibility; so we come in humility, knowing that the least we could do—and by grace have done—is to erect a temple dedicated to the worship of our gracious God, our loving Redeemer and Savior, our Advocate, our God, three in one. Today we honor God and our obedience with a worship experience of thanksgiving for the ending of this debt: the burning of our mortgage. Praise God!

Cornerstone Laying

We come today, for history and posterity to mark and take note of the men and women who led us in the [building or renovation] of this church building. The cornerstone bears the names of: [list all the names on the cornerstone]; and we are grateful to them and to all of you who have made this moment possible, on this date, [month/day/year]. When many of us are no longer on this side of Jordan, this marker will stand as a monument, as a beacon to the world that a group of believers on [street name] in [city], erected a building used to witness to the world that Jesus is Lord, and worthy of praise. Today, we make a formal profession of faith, hope, and commitment represented by this historical moment.

Groundbreaking

Today we begin another chapter or segment of our understanding of God's plan and will for members of [church name or mission]. This body began in [year] as an idea, a dream. [Insert the key names of people and how the church began.] In that same spirit of service and desire to spread God's work and minister to the [city name] community, we come today to break the ground where we will construct our new edifice [offices, educational facility, and so on]. We prayerfully anoint this ground as hallowed and sacred. May we be faithful to support the completion of this dream. In Jesus' name, we bless this ground, the dreamers, and the dream.

Welcome

We welcome you with open, happy hearts and gratitude, as we celebrate the [mortgage burning or cornerstone laying or groundbreaking] of [church name]. We have sought the Lord, worked long, hard hours, offered many prayers, made extensive plans, and engaged in fund-raising on our journey that brings us here today. We do not regret the time or effort required to realize our dream. We testify to the work and commitment. We invite you to celebrate our vision and our work with us.

On behalf of our pastor, officers, and members, we welcome you to join with the singing, praising, and sharing. Let us all lift up our voices to the Lord. Let us all be renewed and be open to God's great and powerful vision for us. Let us see this [mortgage burning or cornerstone laying or groundbreaking] as a symbol of a new life and the opportunity to grow and be redeemed in Christ Jesus. Welcome to our church and our hearts. Welcome to a new day and new dreams. Welcome to life! Welcome.

Prayer

Lord, you have said, "On this rock I will build my church, and the gates of Hades will not prevail against it" (Matt. 16:18b). We praise you for the gifts of yourself, the grounds and places of worship, the abilities and means that enable frail human beings to participate in this process. O Lord, you are so great and magnificent. From the beginning of time through the times of our biblical ancestors; from New Testament times until today—you have created and given us much in love.

Lord, we thank you for your gifts of unconditional love. We thank you that you always are reconciling us to you. Gracious Creator, through your covenants with us, through the prophets, through Jesus, you continue to bring us back into relationships. For these acts and so many more, you are worthy of praise. In honor of you, dear Architect of the universe, we [*burn this mortgage or lay this cornerstone or break this ground*].

Lord, help us to be willing to do what you require: "to do justice, and to love kindness, and to walk humbly with [our] God" (Mic. 6:8). Teach us to respect and honor you and all that is dedicated to your glory, including ourselves. Amen.

Litany

LEADER: Lift up your heads, ye everlasting doors. We are here in honor and praise of God, in dedication of the [*burning of this mortgage or the historical marking of this event or this hallowed space*].

PEOPLE: **Just as "the LORD builds up Jerusalem; [and] gathers the outcasts of Israel", so the Lord allows us to build, pay for, and mark our Christian witness in [*name of city*] on these corners of [*street names*].**

LEADER: The Lord has blessed us mightily and calls us to praise and worship; to teach and preach the Word, to gather those who have become outcasts, to help those who suffer, and to minister to those in need. The need for the Word in the world and building Christian community support our efforts today.

PEOPLE: **Gracious Lord, as we rededicate ourselves and come to [*burn this mortgage or lay this cornerstone or break this ground*] to further the work of [*church name*], we do this in obedience, out of love, and in praise.**

ALL: In humble gratitude, we do this act of dedication, in accord with the scriptures as homage and praise of God's sanctuary and firmament, for God's mighty deeds and greatness, with trumpet, lute, harp, tambourine, and dance; for everything that breathes is called to praise the Lord!

Vow of Commitment

On this special day, we remember those who held this dream long before many of us were born. We offer thanks for those pastors and members instrumental in bringing us to this great day. In the spirit of self-giving and growth, we rededicate ourselves to God's vision of the church and of our activity in the world.

Mortgage Burning

As we burn this mortgage, we offer thanks and we recommit our lives and means to the ministry of [*church name*]. We rejoice to be free of debt. We vow to continue to work for the church in spiritual, ministerial, and financial ways. We commit to the upkeep of this facility. Lord, help us stay true to your Word; to invite others to come and partake of the gospel; and to develop programming for our church that will fully use these buildings to your glory.

Cornerstone Laying

As we lay this stone on this building, we lift our voices in praise and thanksgiving. This stone symbolizes the foundation anchored in Christ Jesus and the "roots" of all the members of the [*church name*] family. Jesus Christ is the foundation of the church: Jesus calls us, softly and tenderly, to be in unity, rooted in love. The cornerstone is the concrete example of our spiritual anchoring in God. As we seal this cornerstone, this "rock" onto our building, let us celebrate that Jesus is the solid rock on which we stand.

Groundbreaking

As prophets and priests of old built altars to the glory of God, today we break ground to raise a house of God. We lift shovels of dirt to symbolize the start of actual building. May each new hole, each nail, each fixture, board, carpet, and seat put in place be done to God's glory. May we remain as enthusiastic as we are today throughout the construction of our new building. As we build a building, Lord, let us do our part to build you up through word and deed in the life of the church as we witness to the world.

Suggested Colors

Purple and pink are the suggested colors for projects related to building. Purple symbolizes power, high energy, deep feeling, spirituality, self-esteem, and abundance. Pink symbolizes gentleness, high spirits, quality, warmth, and welcome.

Scriptures

But may all who seek you rejoice and be glad in you; may those who love your salvation say continually, "Great is the LORD!" (Ps. 40:16)

"So that this may be a sign among you. When your children ask in time to come, 'What do those stones mean to you?' then you shall tell them that the waters of the Jordan were cut off in front of the ark of the covenant of the LORD. When it crossed over the Jordan, the waters of the Jordan were cut off. So these stones shall be to the Israelites a memorial forever." (Josh. 4:6-7)

Jesus said to them, "Have you never read in the scriptures: 'The stone that the builders rejected has become the cornerstone; this was the Lord's doing, and it is amazing in our eyes'?" (Matt. 21:42)

"Yet the Most High does not dwell in houses made with human hands; as the prophet says, 'Heaven is my throne, and the earth is my footstool. What kind of house will you build for me, says the Lord, or what is the place of my rest? Did not my hands make all these things?'" (Acts 7:48-50)

Poem of Reflection

WHAT MEAN THESE STONES?

Groundbreakings
Cornerstone layings
Mortgage burnings
Hallowed spaces
Stones and spaces
Dedicated
to the
Worship of God.

Out of debt
Marking history
Shoveling earth
Movement toward
Owning, naming, building
Sanctuaries for worship
For celebrating abundant life.

We build
Not for form or fashion
But for God—
Places to meet and greet
To teach and do outreach
What mean these stones?
The Lord is in this Holy Place:
Let us praise.

CHURCH BUILDING DEDICATION*

Occasion

Church building dedications celebrate God's gift of a new dwelling to a church family. The church, the Body of Christ, comes together in a building that symbolizes a gathered community of families, parents or guardians, husbands, wives, grandparents, children, other relatives, pastors, officers, and team builders. They are called together in love, to grow collectively and individually, to fulfill God's vision of peace for them on earth. In ancient Israel, people grouped together as families, clans, tribes, and a nation. Family, the smallest unit, consisted of husband and wife, all children (single or married), servants and their families, any single relatives without a father, and any visitors who lived tempo-

---

*This service works for the dedication of a new church facility, or a renovation project.

rarily with the family. A clan was a group of related families. A tribe was a group of clans who traced their heritage from a common ancestor; and a nation, the largest unit, was led by a king. All groups related to one another and to God. Everything was a part of the reality of God and this community's obedience.

Modern families take many forms: single or two parents with one, many, natural, adopted, or foster children; singles or couples with no children; extended families of aunts, uncles, cousins, and grandparents. [*Church name*] includes all these family forms. Long before Solomon built the Temple at Jerusalem, families worshiped God in a family setting. Today we celebrate a sacred place, a place we call home. Our church home is a place where we celebrate God with others, take refuge, grow, give shelter and nurture to others, and are loved as a faith community.

Today, we honor this God-centered church home, ordained as a sanctuary of love. We come to bless the contents and all persons who serve and come here. We anoint this house as a blessed haven of worship and peace. We bless the pastoral, education, community service, and outreach staff, and ask God to keep them safe and bring them renewal. We bless the [*church name*] family and pray that daily we become more Christlike, individually and collectively. We thank God for the vision, the financial support, and the hard work that allows us to be here today. May we each be blessed to worship, work, and serve here for many years. Blessings! All honor, glory, and praise to God!

Welcome

Welcome mats lay at the foot of people's doors, implying that the family welcomes family, neighbors, friends, and even strangers to come to their homes. We the [*church name family*] welcome the pastor(s) [*name of pastor(s)*], pulpit guests, officers, and members of [*church name*], and of our guest churches, and our visiting friends to the dedication of our [*new or renovated*] church home on this most joyous occasion. We invite you to relax and enjoy your visit in Christ Jesus.

We welcome you to celebrate our joy at being in our new church home. God blessed us with the vision and the means to be here; God especially blesses us today with your presence, with health, joy, and peace. We deeply appreciate your presence, prayers, and best wishes as we celebrate all that is good, beautiful, and true. We welcome you, in the name of Christ Jesus, to celebrate the times in history when our ancestors could not openly worship and own property. Let us never forget their faith in God, their perseverance, their ability to survive, their humor, and their creativity at church, at home, and on the job: praising, praying, working, starting new ministries and their own businesses, spreading the Word; using what they had, by God's grace, to make what they needed.

Welcome to our God-given church home! Be refreshed, feel good! When you depart, know that we are your friends. When you talk to Jesus, do whisper a prayer for us!

Prayer

Gracious God, the architect of the universe, the builder of all that is good and perfect: we honor you and your magnificent handiwork throughout creation. O Faithful One, we praise you for the ideas you place within us that result in beautiful designs and structures. Lord, you are so gracious and loving. God, you so honor us by blessing us with creativity, knowledge, and strength. You blessed King Solomon with the wisdom and riches to build a house, a temple for your name. You have allowed [*name of church*] to build this house in your name, for our use. We ask you, O Everlasting One, to bless us with the insight to dedicate this edifice and our hearts to your service.

Gracious Creator, we are grateful that you have allowed us to see this day. We rejoice in your love and wisdom. You created this church family out of love and obedience to you. You have always provided for us. Help us to live honorably and to love and provide for others as a witness to you. Let this house be a house of prayer. Lord, may our church family stand together, held firmly by grace, bonded in faith, and united in love. Help us to honor and respect you, to honor and respect our neighbor, and to honor and respect ourselves.

Teach us to live each day as a household of faith. May each brick or stone, each slab of wood, each pipe and electrical fixture be rightfully placed and withstand the elements. May this Body of Christ be a beacon to those who need a redeeming vision, a way station, a ray of hope, an oasis. May we stand together as a church family as the house stands anchored here. Amen.

Litany

LEADER: In prayer and song, we rejoice. We thank God for the opportunity to honor and praise God, in dedicating the home of the [*church family name*].

PEOPLE: **God promised to give Abraham land and children, and to make him a great nation. The Lord brought Ruth and Naomi from famine and emptiness to a land of plenty, to build a new family. God brings us today to rededicate ourselves and our church home in [*name of city*] on these corners of [*street names*].**

LEADER: The Lord calls us to love one another and to honor our divinely given covenant here at [*church name*] as we daily serve God through what we say and do.

PEOPLE: **Loving God, we dedicate ourselves, this sanctuary, these grounds and facilities, as an act of praise and obedience. Lord, we know this is your house, for you** made it possible. Again, we offer praise and thanksgiving.

ALL: In grateful appreciation, we place before you this church home, as a haven of love and Christian nurture for us and [name of city/community], to edify you, to do that which is pleasing in your sight. Hallelujah!

Vow of Commitment

On this special day, we offer thanks for all those who make our vision a reality. In the spirit of joy and celebration, we dedicate ourselves and our church home to building loving community and relationships between one another under the will and activity of God.

We pledge to be good stewards. with the Lord's gift of this facility comes much responsibility. We are charged to tithe and support our building fund, maintain the upkeep on the property, and share love in our church home. We honor the trust that God places in us to be firm in our commitment. May this building and the grounds be used to the service and honor of God.

We pledge that each service and activity be done in thanksgiving. When these doors open, while we are here, we vow to lift up the Lord's name daily, to spend time studying God's Word, and to remember that this house is God's house. We promise to hold firm in the faith of Christ Jesus, as the Lord is our Helper.

Suggested Colors

Pink and blue are the suggested colors for a church building dedication. Pink symbolizes gentleness, high spirits, quality, warmth, and welcome. Blue represents serenity, work, space, royalty, and unity.

Scriptures

Do not be afraid when some become rich, when the wealth of their houses increases. (Ps. 49:16)

Their houses are safe from fear, and no rod of God is upon them. (Job 21:9)

And if a house is divided against itself, that house will not be able to stand. (Mark 3:25)

For every house is built by someone, but the builder of all things is God. (Heb. 3:4)

Poem of Reflection

OUR CHURCH HOUSE, OUR HOME

The steeple stands tall
Rosebushes look grand, windows sparkle so
The kids play in a box of sand;
Our new church house is roomy
A special place for us all
What I like the best is God's peaceful rest.

Plans and sweat and thought went into this God's house.
We prayed, we dreamed.
Our delight so present on our face;
The paint is fresh the carpet new
The lawn grows 'neath the dew.
We're blessed delighted as can be
What makes us happy is that we're here together with thee.

Dear God we thank and praise you for all you've done for us.
You've given us your house and home,
A joyous, spiritual place to roam;
Midst family and friends
To learn, to grow, to teach
To share, to love, to reach.

We lift our heads and hearts
To you, great God and Friend
We sit, sing, laugh, and pray,
As we gather in your name.
We thank you, O Mighty One,
Your house is our home.

CHOIR
ANNIVERSARY DAY

Occasion

Queen Deborah and Barak sang as they led Israel and blessed the Lord (Judg. 5). Singing is an act of praise in which individuals and congregations make music in joyful noise to the Lord. Church choirs are groups of people that make music in adoration, praise, and glory of God. Choirs are an integral part of the worship service and the life of the church. Today we rejoice and celebrate the gifts and contributions of the [*name of the choir*]. Today we offer three challenges: First, we thank the choir and challenge them to continue to grow in God's grace. Second, we challenge those musically gifted who have not yet become a part of [*church name*] choirs to participate. God gave you a talent. You multiply that talent a hundred-fold when you sing. Those who sing once, pray twice. Third, we challenge the congregation to sing with and pray for the spiritual well-being, anointing, and ministry of [*name of choir*].

As we honor this angelic chorus, we pray for their continued renewal. We pray that God anoints [*names of musicians*] as they direct, accompany, teach, inspire, and serve. May each note they sing radiate with Spirit-filled power from on high. Our praise and thanks to God for the opportunity to participate in and to listen to [*name of choir*] during their [*number*] years of service to [*church name*] and to the [*city or community*].

Welcome

Make a joyful noise unto the Lord, all you lands, all you people everywhere! With many voices, instruments, and song, we welcome each of you to the [*number*] annual choir anniversary celebration.

To the pastor, officers, members, and friends of [*church name*], greetings and joy! The [*choir name*] members are blessed by your presence and are grateful for the opportunity to lift up the Lord's name in song. Serving you today is our ministry. Feel free to join in with a hand clap, a nod of the head, or a great Amen!

We come before you in awe of God and of the many talents and musical gifts bestowed upon us. We rejoice that you are here to share in this service of the Word and song. Just as God created birds of song to serenade the divinely created handiwork we call the world, God has given us many songs to sing. Psalm 150 tells us all about praising God:

Where: In God's sanctuary and mighty firmament!

Why: For God's mighty deeds and surpassing greatness!

How: With lute and harp; tambourine and dance; strings and pipes, clanging and loud clashing cymbals!

Let everything that breathes praise God! Welcome to praise time!

Prayer

O great Creator of sound and Conductor of heavenly symphonies! O Ancient of Days, how magnificent and eloquent you are! Every song, every musical work—combination of sound and silence, of melody and rhythm—every created utterance is yours.

Gracious Lord, we thank you for the beauty and majesty of all song and for those who have sung praises to your most holy name. We thank you for the gift of standing in the traditions of choirs like the Fisk Jubilee Singers, the Hampton College Choir, the Walter Hawkins Singers, and the Edwin Hawkins Singers, and the Gospel Workshop of America. We offer praises for the great compositions and arrangements by Thomas A. Dorsey, Virgie C. DeWitty, William Dawson, Roberta Martin, Sally Martin, James Cleveland, Mary Lou Williams, and Aretha Franklin.

We shout with glad hosannas for the choral and part singing of The Mighty Clouds of Joy, the Winans Family, Take 6, and the many senior and sanctuary choirs, gospel choruses, community mass choirs, ensembles, youth, young adult, and children's choirs that sing the Word, worldwide.

Blessed Director of all life, fix our hearts, minds, bodies, and spirits that we might always sing for your glory. Help us to be joyful, willing vessels that carry healing, inspiring sound. Let the meditations of our hearts, the messages of our mouths, and the proclamations of our lives in Christ Jesus be acceptable in your sight. Amen.

Litany

LEADER: How blessed we are! God has graced us with bountiful gifts of song.

PEOPLE: **We receive these gifts from God, and in joy, respond with musical offering back to God.**

LEADER: With psalmists, poets, singers, and composers, who have left us a legacy more valuable than gold and precious gems.

PEOPLE: **We lift our voices and play our instruments through God's graciousness, as a worship covenant in obedience to praise.**

LEADER: Sing the song of salvation; for God is with us as Christ Jesus, incarnated love, that gives us freedom to live. God allows us to create, empowered by the Holy Spirit.

PEOPLE: **In awe of God, we sing hallelujah, as we march to Zion, that blessed Jerusalem, telling the world about this, that we are blessed.**

ALL: **Hosanna, hosanna in the highest! We sing, we praise, we worship in music ministry. Hosanna, hosanna, hosanna!**

Vow of Commitment

On this blessed occasion, we rejoice and offer thanks for the opportunity to serve the Lord, our congregation, and the community through song. In love and humility, we devote ourselves and our gifts to the feeding and creative nurture of all through the ministry of music.

We take a vow of excellence. We will be good students, attentive listeners, and will reflect on singing and living the messages we perform. We will continue to examine our role in the ministry of [*church name*]. We stand together in faith and in hope that each time we offer music we do so in awe of God, with a godly heart and spirit. We understand that solo and group performances are done to God's edification and not for selfish gains. We pledge to cooperate with the musicians and directors by being on time for rehearsals, preparing and learning our music, and being willing to sing, in season and out of season. We thank and bless God for this marvelous opportunity.

We recommit ourselves to God's ministry of music at [*church name*]. When we don our robes and take our seats in the choir, we come in thanksgiving as God's messengers. We pledge our support and time to a musical ministry of reconciliation, knowing that a song we sing may soothe a broken heart, strengthen one who is weak, or bring a sin-sick soul to Christ Jesus. We sing mightily and stand firm in the Lord.

Suggested Colors

Orange and purple are the suggested colors for a choir anniversary celebration. Orange symbolizes the earth, autumn, warmth, fruitfulness, cheerfulness, and richness. Purple represents royalty, penitence, power, self-esteem, and depth of feeling.

Scriptures

O [our] strength, [we] will sing praises to you, for you, O God, are [our] fortress, the God who shows [us] steadfast love. (Ps. 59:17)

Sing and rejoice, O daughter Zion! For lo, I will come and dwell in your midst, says the LORD. (Zech. 2:10)

As [Jesus] was now approaching the path down from the Mount of Olives, the whole multitude of the disciples began to praise God joyfully with a loud voice for all the deeds of power that they had seen. (Luke 19:37)

About midnight Paul and Silas were praying and singing hymns to God, and the prisoners were listening to them. Suddenly there was an earthquake, so violent that the foundations of the prison were shaken; and immediately all the doors were opened and everyone's chains were unfastened. (Acts 16:25-26)

Poem of Reflection

GOD'S VOICE

Sunday after Sunday
We lift our voices in anthems, gospels, hymns.
To send a message of hope and good news
As we testify about
The Savior's love for us;
And people are touched
For the soloist and chorus
Sang with the voice of God.

With the mighty strains of the organ:
Resounding great ocean waves—
With the lilting tones of the sopranos:
Soaring majestic birds o'er meadows—
With mellow, soulful wails of the altos:
Moving elegant lionesses watching their young
With the rock-steady action of the piano:
Galloping colts in fields of green—
With the clarion swells of tenors:
Gliding eagles above mountain peaks—
With the sonorous depth of basses:
Swimming graceful whales midst the ocean blue—
A completed scenario
Of beauteous sound and silence
Of creation made eternal
Before beginnings
Listen, for a jubilant song
Is the voice of God.

BLACK HISTORY CELEBRATION

Occasion

Carter G. Woodson knew the importance of knowing one's self and knowing one's history. Thus he began the celebration of Black history. Today we celebrate Black history. Let us extend this occasion to a daily celebration of who we are and whose we are.

We are noble, elegant creatures of God. We have a past, a present, and a future in Christ Jesus. Millions have gone before us. Many have taught, produced, shared, and cared. Many of our ancestors died during the Middle Passage, and now rest in the Atlantic Ocean. Many of our ancestors arrived to these shores and, with a God that helped them to make a way out of no way, managed to withstand the cruelties and rigors of slavery. They were creative and smart. They took a remnant of their African culture and merged it with what they gleaned from Western culture; and this indigenous Black culture flourished on American soil. The knowledge of our history roots us deeply, with the legacy of a creative, ingenious, surviving, God-centered people. History shows us possibility and builds community.

We honor the persons and recall the events of African American history. We recognize the historical heritage of [*name of city*] and of [*church name*]. We pray that God will help us to learn about and learn from the past, to better live with self-esteem and self-awareness today, to better prepare for the time when the future tomorrow becomes today.

We salute the historic efforts of persons dedicated to the liberation of all people. We take our hats off to abolitionists and freedom fighters throughout history. We salute ourselves during this [*number*] annual Black History Month. May there come a time when the interaction and empowerment of all society reaches a point where we all celebrate Black history daily.

Welcome

The hymn writer says, "We've a story to tell to the nations!" We have many stories to tell about God and the Bible, about ourselves, our culture, our realities. Telling stories helps us to build community, we reflect the lives of one another and celebrate the similarities and differences without hating or controlling others, or have them control us. Today we celebrate the sharing of stories of an African American experience.

To the pastor, officers, members, and friends of [*church name*], greetings and blessings in Jesus' name! We celebrate the heritage of your family and our collective families. We honor the stories and traditions of the African American experience in [*name of city*]. We bless God for the history of [*church name*] and our ministry to our church family, friends, and one another. We welcome you to join us in honoring the many accomplishments and contributions of African Americans to our lives and to this country: parents, pastors, professors, poets, inventors, intellectual giants, freedom instigators, musicians, medicine men and women, astronauts, athletes, lawyers and legislators, and all other persons who help create the quilted fabric of African American lifestyle and history.

One of the ways we know God is through God's acts in history: with the Hebrew children and the early church. God continues to act with us and for us. What we do today is our history-making process. Welcome to our celebration. We invite you to learn more about *who* you are and *whose* you are. Again, welcome!

Prayer

O God of life and history, who acted in the beginning and acts today; we praise your eternal mercy and justice that sustains us in our strength and frailty. We thank you for the lives of slaves, who praised your name despite the tyranny that oppressed them. We thank you for those who always protested injustice, and rallied for change and transformation in the home, church, and society.

Help us to name the evils of the past and present. Empower us, O God, to never deny who we are, and to see our physicalness as beauty. Help us, dear author and finisher of our faith, to have a true sense of the accomplishments of African Americans and to have a vision of possibility about all we can be and do. Teach us that beauty is being and action. We are beautiful because we are created in God's image; we are beautiful as we respect ourselves and others.

O Redeemer, we thank you for life, health, and strength. We thank you for the world, for ideas, for creativity, for family, for ourselves, for today. Lord, help us to live today, this day, as special and extraordinary in an ordinary way. Help us to live this day so well, that when the history of this day is written, we can hear God say about today: "Well done, my good and faithful servant!"

Litany

LEADER: Holy, holy, holy Lord, God of life and history.

PEOPLE: **Heaven and earth are full of your glory, from the beginning of human society through today. How great and glorious are you, dear Lord. How great is your handiwork.**

LEADER: The greatness of your creation shapes the life and community stories of our world, our ancestors, our families, ourselves. We celebrate, this day, the magnificence of the African American contributions to those stories.

PEOPLE: **We thank God and those inspired women and men who have taught us our own history. We are grateful for those who follow in the footsteps of Carter G. Woodson, historian, architect, and chief celebrant of Black History, and Maulana Karenga, writer and driving force behind Kwanza. They remind us to study ourselves and to uphold the community values that are a part of our heritage.**

LEADER: Let us go forth to read and teach ourselves and our children. Let us study about Africa, slavery, and the early African American churches and freedom struggles. Then we can call the roll: Richard Allen, Daniel Payne, and Jarena Lee with the African Methodist Episcopals; Absalom Jones, James Varick, and Christopher Rush with the African Methodist Episcopal Zions; Isaac Lane and Lucius Holsey with the Christian Methodist Episcopal.

PEOPLE: **Nathaniel Paul, Elias C. Morris, and T. Clarkson with African American Baptists; William J. Seymour, C. P. Jones, and C. H. Mason with the Holiness movements and the Church of God in Christ; and Augustus Tolton, first African American priest, and the early members of the African American Catholic Congresses.**

LEADER: We thank and praise God for these named movers and shakers, and hundreds of others, in religious and general educational history, in industry, health care, the arts, sciences, politics, and entertainment for the wealth of knowledge and character they have shared.

PEOPLE: **In thanksgiving and anticipation, O God, we thank you for the gift of these lives and for the blessings of remembering.**

ALL: **We remember the past to build on and live today; we live today in hopeful imagination to provide a story for the future.**

Vow of Commitment

As we celebrate God's gift of story, we remember that we each have a part to play. Our stories reflect God's glimmer of divine grace. Teaching the stories of the past and the stories of our congregation and the community is an opportunity to share our love of the Lord and the gospel message. With eager anticipation, we devote ourselves to the complete salvation and liberation of [*church name*] members and our community through sharing gospel and community stories that can empower and strengthen ourselves and one another.

We pledge ourselves to the well-being of all people. We see part of our educational ministry as an opportunity to look closely in our past and learn about our ancestors. We can continue to liberate our families and friends as we keep aware of current events and how they affect the social and political health of our local and church community.

We vow to share our history of overcoming obstacles with those less fortunate. We stand together to tell stories of reconciliation and forgiveness. We look to God's activity of healing and loving us when we cannot love ourselves; to remember how we are to love, as our daily living creates history. We commit our time and energies and gifts to forming solidarity in our extended family communities; to lessening violence; to being mentors and good listeners; to daily reflection about the integrity of our stories and the living of our lives.

Suggested Colors

Red, black, and green are the colors for a Black history celebration. Red stands for love, living blood, emotion, ardor, strife, anger, passion, and warmth. Green symbolizes life, love, freshness, growth, perspective, and visibility. Black symbolizes solidarity, strength, power, infinity, freshness, healing, peace, visibility, growth, and the divine.

Scriptures

No weapon that is fashioned against [us] shall prosper, and [we] shall confute every tongue that rises against [us] in judgment. This is the heritage of the servants of the LORD and their vindication from me, says the LORD. (Isa. 54:17)

Let bronze be brought from Egypt; let Ethiopia hasten to stretch out its hands to God. (Ps. 68:31)

"For I was hungry and you gave me food, I was thirsty and you gave me something to drink, I was a stranger and you welcomed me, I was naked and you gave me clothing, I was sick and you took care of me, I was in prison and you visited me." (Matt. 25:35-36)

Therefore, since we are surrounded by so great a cloud of witnesses, let us also lay aside every weight and the sin that clings so closely, and let us run with perseverance the race that is set before us, looking to Jesus the pioneer and perfecter of our faith. (Heb. 12:1-2a)

Poem of Reflection

BLACK, BOLD, BEAUTIFUL

Blackness as strength
Embraces
Shapes
Teaches us.
Blackness as pigmentation
Colors
Delights
Identifies us.
Blackness as power
Strengthens
Solidifies
Ennobles us.

The awesomeness of God amidst Blackness is:
So profound that we miss it;
So massive that others fear it;
So wonderful that others envy it;
So unique that others need to destroy it.
Must we miss, fear, envy, or destroy ourselves?

The symphonic hues of Blackness in history
Weave the melodies
Cast majestically in
All the movements and
Days of our lives:
Yesterday, today, tomorrow,
If we love Blackness today.
His-story, her-story, our-story,
Magnificent Blackness personified.
Can I get a witness?